Coppa Monte

2000

Author
John A. Mango

Copyright © 2000 by John A. Mango

All rights reserved. No part of this book shall be reproduced or transmitted in any form or by any means, electronic, mechanical, magnetic, photographic including photocopying, recording or by any information storage and retrieval system, without prior written permission of the publisher. No patent liability is assumed with respect to the use of the information contained herein. Although every precaution has been taken in the preparation of this book, the publisher and author assume no responsibility for errors or omissions. Neither is any liability assumed for damages resulting from the use of the information contained herein.

ISBN 0-7414-0464-8

Published by:

Infinity Publishing.com
519 West Lancaster Avenue
Haverford, PA 19041-1413
Info@buybooksontheweb.com
www.buybooksontheweb.com
Toll-free (877) BUY BOOK
Local Phone (610) 520-2500
Fax (610) 519-0261

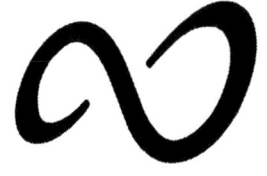

Printed in the United States of America
Printed on Recycled Paper
Published November-2000

Dedication
Especially to my mother and father, who spent their whole adult life, seeing that my sisters and I received the best that they could provide us. Also to my uncles and aunts and all the Italians who came to America for paving a road for us, the first-born Italian American.

Acknowledgements

Thanks to mother's brother Filippo who provided the early history for this story.

Thanks to my wife Pia for all the help in writing the Italian language inserts.

Recalling details of the events in my life was relatively easy. Over time (eight years), as I wrote about each incident, more details came to mind. Thanks to my sister Anna, who reminded me of the problems dad had with doctors in the diagnosis of Giovannina's medical problems.

Many thanks to my dear sister Marie, who in our discussions before her death in 1969 was instrumental in providing and clarifying details of events of the 1920s and early 1930s for me.

Many thanks to Doris Deutsch of Trempealeau, Wisconsin. She was visiting California just when I needed help before this story could be completed.

It was difficult remembering the details my mother told of events in the early part of the century. Some stories she told many times over the years. However, I didn't listen well enough. When I sat at the computer to write this narrative, I wished I had started this before she died. Or, that I had listened more attentively.

I owe a debt of gratitude to her, my three children, and all the folks who are remembered on these pages.

jm

Forward

Coppa Monte, up the mountain, is an appropriate title for a book about immigrants coming to America. While it meant working the land up in the mountains for those early people in Italy, it also meant carving out a new life in a new land for those who left Italy

Promises of wealth and a life of ease prompted hundreds of thousands of people to leave their homelands. Little did they know their lives would continue to have struggles, disappointments, with very little ease. It certainly was a time to scale the mountains of hard work and sacrifice. But it also produced people of pride, people of great dedications, and above all, people who knew the meaning of family.

John Mango's book, *Coppa Monte* tells a poignant story of his ancestors; their reasons for leaving Italy and their lives in America, a land not filled with milk and honey. He tells of their personal loss, the death of family and friends, the depth of poverty, and the heights of gladness as hope fill their hearts.

As he draws the scenes of their arrival we can see these young men in old New York, full of wonder and awe at the bustling city. From his great-uncles and his own parents, we gather a perfect picture of one family's acclimation to America.

The intense battle to succeed against adverse conditions is almost heroic. The loss of a child so dreadful that even in later years, brings tears to the writer, and is shared by the reader. Even more so is the unselfish act of Marie, whose only concern was to bring some joy at Christmas with her little gifts. And like the Gifts of the Magi, had no gift for herself.

But life goes on. The family becomes more affluent. The next generation takes over, and the following generation finally realizes the fruits of the labors of those who went before. It is a heritage we all share with our own ancestors who built this country.

This is an important story; one that should not be lost, but savored for its contribution to the formation of this country. It is only one of the many stories of those wonderful, gritty, proud, dedicated people we call immigrants.

Doris Deutsch

Contents

	Introduction	v
1	Coppa Monte	1
2	Finding work in America	10
3	Back home in Italy	18
4	The Moiano Mango Family	22
5	More of the second generation comes to America	31
6	Peppino (Giuseppe) goes to America	35
7	The Great War brings changes	41
8	Giuseppe & Maddalena	44
9	Maddalena and daughters visit Italy	58
10	Working on the Erie Railroad	61
11	Troubles on the Erie Railroad	64

Contents

12	The Great Depression	66
13	Giovannina becomes ill	70
14	Jobs lost on the Erie Railroad	74
15	Misfortunes	81
16	Settling in Our New Home	85
17	The final Days of Giovannina	92
18	Food Supplies during The Great Depression	95
19	Another Christmas	99
20	Discipline and Education	103
21	Memories 1930s	107
22	Summertime	111
23	Move again, and again	114

Contents

24	Hornell and Prosperity	125
25	Carefree Teenager	132
26	U. S. enters the war	137
27	Growing up	149
28	World War Two ends	158
	Appendix	161
	Index	163

Chapter

1 *Coppa Monte*

Writing a book about Italians in America began as I researched my own beginnings. Memories of a childhood long gone caused me to drive east, back to the scene of those early years. When my wife Pia and I, drove from our home in California to those eastern cities, I secretly hoped to recapture my childhood feelings and memories.

I vividly remember the years of the Great Depression in Susquehanna Pennsylvania, and the hardships my family faced. I also recall the Erie Railroad and the part it played in our family, and many others in that small Pennsylvania community.

Susquehanna was a division terminal. It had repair shops, a roundhouse, coal pockets, and both westbound and eastbound yards. On the other side of the Susquehanna River, and west of town at the eastbound yards, pusher engines were added to the eastbound freight trains.

The freights strained to attain the speed needed to make it nine miles up the hill to Gulf Summit. When they reached the station, they were already going 50 mph. Even though we lived four blocks up the mountain from the station, we could hear the eastbound freight trains leaving town. The slow chug, chug, chug, coming across the valley as they labored to push the freight trains over the hill, still lingers in my memory.

My childhood home on Prospect Street is still there, although it's been remodeled more than once through the years. Fill dirt covers the well where we used to get cool water to drink. The big red barn where we kept a cow, and stored dad's tools, was torn down years ago. Weeds cover the garden area where vegetables, so necessary during the depression, were grown. Washington Street School still stands, as does St. John's Catholic Church. But it was at the church cemetery that old feelings surfaced as I remembered my little sister who died and was buried there, so many years ago.

Susquehanna is still a small community with a population of 2,500, which is about the same as it had so long ago. When the railroad left, Susquehanna failed to thrive and grow. The Erie Railroad no longer exists. Its successor Conrail, runs a couple of freight trains each way daily. There is nothing to indicate that this was a thriving railroad community in the early part of the 20th century.

The town of Hornell, New York, 149 miles to the other end of the division, was our next stop. My old house on Front Street is gone. The River Street bridge is old and dilapidated, though I remember when it was built. Bryant school, where I once attended, looks entirely different. I would have liked to thank my 6th grade teacher Miss Kemp, because she was a special person in my life, but I can't. She's just another part of a childhood memory.

The Erie Railroad roundhouse is gone but the back shops are still there and from the outside it looks the same. The passenger station is boarded up and abandoned. So many changes, so many people gone, I sadly realized that I could never recapture those childhood feelings, not even for a moment.

I remember well my Italian heritage. Almost 70 years have passed, but I remember my parents and their friends sharing experiences of leaving their hometowns in Italy. They left hardships in the old country only to encounter even more problems here with the Great Depression and two World Wars. They boarded the ships with high hopes for a better life. They came to America, and through very hard work, succeeded in making a better life for all of us, the first generation of Italian Americans.

My story, *Coppa Monte*, starts with a visit to a small Italian village, not far from Naples, where my parents and grandparents lived.

The year is 1883. The scene is a tiny and obscure Italian village, Moiano, nestled beneath Tuburno Mountain, which looms 1,980 feet above it. Moiano is 21 miles from Naples. It is easily found by heading 18 miles northeast from Naples to the village of Arpaia, then three more miles straight north.

The terrain of the village and surrounding area is one of rolling hills. In winter the snow covered caps of the Apennine Mountains can be seen in the east. The climate of Moiano is similar to southern California. There is enough rain during the growing season (March-November), to sustain many food crops.

Dusty roads lead to the village square where the well, which supplies fresh water for the 400 inhabitants, is located. Small stone huts dot the countryside, but the agricultural land is located *coppa monte* (up the mountain), where the rocky soil is fertile and rich. It is *coppa monte*, where the farmers of Moiano eke out a meager living raising grains and vegetables.

There was nothing exceptional about this village; it had the usual percentage of petty thieves, wife beaters, child abusers and drunks. The important part was that everyone knew who these people were. Primarily, because there was nothing of great value to steal or extort from anyone in town, the feared mano nera (black hand) was absent.

The only doctor in town had to compete with "mal occhio" (evil eye) rituals and many other local cures. There was no dentist, but one day every month, two men (who called themselves dentists) arrived in the town square on a two-wheel cart pulled by a "ciuccio" (jackass). The cart carried a supply of wine and one chair.

Customers who bravely lined up were given a glass of wine. Taking turns, each was seated in the chair when one "dentist" held the patient's head, while the other extracted the ailing tooth. On those days you could hear the screaming and wailing all over town, according to my mother.

The town had one small stone school building with three elementary grades. The prevailing opinion in Moiano was that schooling did not teach boys the skills to work the land *coppa monte,* nor teach girls how to sew, cook, keep house, or raise children. Also, the children's help was needed *coppa monte.* Thus, only a child who was physically weak, or sick, or the children of the few wealthy families were sent to school.

Parents were fiercely proud of their children. They instilled in them a belief in God, and reared them as good Catholics. Attending Mass every Sunday was usually a family affair. Children were free to play after church, while men went to the cantina, to talk and drink.

Also on Sunday afternoon women could be seen grooming their long hair that went halfway down their backs. After washing and combing it, each woman fashioned one long braid down her back, rolled it into a bun and pinned it on the back of her head.

Parents taught their children to respect all adults and to call them Zia and Zio (Aunt and Uncle). A family friend named Maria was "Zia Maria" to the young child.

(Note: those from Moiano dropped the vowels from the end of many words and names. Moiano was pronounced "Moi-on," paisano became "pai-saan." Names such as Giovanni became "Giovon", Giuseppe became "Giusepp" Zia, and Zio became "Zi." For that reason in this tale Zia and Zio are referred to as Zi).

Cristoforo Colombo, a fellow Italian, sailed from Spain in 1492, intending to find a new route to the Far East. Instead he discovered a new world. Those who followed Colombo to the new world, brought plants cultivated in the old world. Plants cultivated in the new world were taken to the old world. This exchange of vegetables greatly improved the lives on both sides of the ocean.

The major plants introduced to the Europeans were corn, tomatoes and potatoes. The potato was cultivated and readily eaten by the northern European, particularly in Ireland.

In Moiano the potato was called "patan." The common Italian word for potato is "patata." The Moianese disliked the potato. The same land, which may have been used to raise potatoes, produced enough corn, wheat and beans. These crops provided at least as much to eat as a potato crop would. Since it grew well in the soil *coppa monte,* the limited amounts of potatoes that were cultivated were fed to the pigs, thus more families were able to raise pigs.

Once or twice a year a pig was slaughtered. The undesirable parts were retained to make sausage. The rest of the pig was sold and, stipulated as part of each sale, the buyer cured a prosciutto (ham) for the seller. The prosciutto was a delicacy and an important holiday treat.

Selling pigs earned money to buy needed items families could not make or grow.

Tomatoes were eaten fresh or cooked in a sauce with or without meat. Pasta, a southern Italian food for many centuries, went very well with this tomato sauce.

Corn was usually not eaten fresh. It was dried and ground into corn meal. The rest of the corn plant was fed to the cows. Polenta (cooked corn meal) provided more food for family consumption. Furthermore, like wheat flour and beans, corn meal was stored and eaten all year round.

Families had enough flour from harvested wheat crops to make most of their bread and some of the pasta they consumed each year. Spring and summer vegetables were also cultivated for family consumption, even though there was very little space left for gardens. The greater need was to raise as much wheat, corn and beans.

Milk from cows and goats made many varieties of cheese. Raising chickens was important because of the eggs they produced. When a chicken stopped laying eggs it was killed. Chicken soup with homemade noodles was a treat, and always prepared for a sick family member.

Prosperous families had olive trees. At harvest time in the fall they made dark olive oil, both for family consumption and to sell.

In the late summer and early fall, children would sit on branches of a fig tree to gorge themselves of this abundant fruit. Dried figs were a year-round treat. There was sufficient orange, grapefruit, and lemon trees to satisfy the local need for these fruits. Grapes were not only good to eat but dark zinfandel wine was made from them.

At sun-up each morning except Sunday, families left for *coppa monte* to take care of their crops. Homemade bread, with wine and sometimes cheese, was the food and drink that sustained the family during the day.

The increase in edible foods from the crops of corn, tomatoes, and potatoes from the new world, caused the population in southern Italy to steadily increase. By the early 1880s, due to larger families, the male offspring did not inherit enough farmland to support their families.

Therefore, even before the major immigration of southern Italians to America began in the late 1880s, the young men in town began to look for work opportunities elsewhere.

At that time, Argentina and America were the most popular choices for immigration, because they offered many jobs and good pay. Letters written by those who left Italy told of the benefits and opportunities in their new countries. This alone greatly influenced relatives and friends to follow.

After Mass each Sunday morning the young men would meet to play and talk. The choice to which country they would immigrate was the main topic of conversation for many weeks. In late December of 1882, four of the boys immigrated to Argentina.

One Sunday morning, in late February of 1883, before letters began arriving from Argentina, an individual from Arpaia joined the group of boys. He had just returned from America, so he elaborated on the ready availability of jobs and good pay. He said that in six months a person could repay a loan from his parents for ship passage and have saved enough money for the return trip to Italy. He wore a white shirt. At that time, white shirts were rarely seen and only worn by the very rich. This fact alone convinced the boys he was telling the truth. He told the boys a friend of his in America, Giovanni DeAngelo, who lived in Albany, New York, could be their sponsor. He assured them they would surely find work in Albany.

One of the boys, a very gentle young person, who participated in the Sunday meetings, was Giovanni DiPalma, who was destined to become my maternal grandfather. Before he married he dropped the "Di" from his name, because he said his family had lost any nobility they may have had centuries before.

Giovanni's first cousin and best friend was one of the four who had immigrated to Argentina in December. His cousin had made every effort to talk him into joining their group. Giovanni was sympathetic with the boys who immigrated to Argentina and America. He took keen interest in the letters they wrote. In later years he also immigrated to America and regretted he had not done so earlier.

Another Giovanni, Giovanni Mango who was my paternal grandfather, listened to all the talk of leaving Italy. His cynical response was that those who decided to immigrate were fools to believe what this person from Arpaia said, and fools to expect anything but misery and hard work in America. He had a small plot of land *coppa monte* and was secure in Moiano. He made no effort to wish his departing peers "Buona fortuna" (good fortune) nor did he appear to miss them after they left.

Another young man, Angelo Oropallo, considered making the trip to America. However, he was not ready to join the younger group. Angelo was in his late 20s, and had three little children. Supporting his young family was becoming more difficult and he privately thought he would eventually have to go to America. Several years later, in 1889, he immigrated to New York and worked there for four years before returning home. Angelo's sister Francesca, married Giovanni Mango, and she became my father's mother.

Fiore, Angelo's younger brother, decided not to make the trip to America at that time. Had he gone to America then, it may have changed his, and his future family's entire life. Although he did not leave when Angelo did, he left in 1903 and abandoned his wife and four little children in Moiano. His story continues in a later chapter.

The northern Italians had been immigrating to America in small numbers since the late 1860s. In 1880, those emigrating from southern Italy greatly out-numbered their counterparts from the north. From 1890 through 1922, interrupted only by World War One, this migration numbered in the hundreds of thousands each of those years.

The immigrating southern Italians were primarily single males. Each intended to come to America, accumulate money, and return to Italy to marry and raise their families. At first many of them did just that. Later, around the turn of the century, they returned to Italy only to marry their Italian sweethearts then return with them to raise their families in America.

Of the ten Moiano boys who decided to go to America, only the parents of five of them had the $30.00 needed for the one-way fare. I know the names of two of the five; they were Angelo Saccone, and Ferdinando Pepe. All the mothers and fathers, with heavy hearts, tearfully waved goodbye, and proclaimed "Dio vi benedice, scrivi presto" (God bless you, and write soon). Each boy held one small cloth bag of personal belongings. They sat in Zi Michele's (Ferdinando's father's) donkey cart as he told the ciuccio to move. Three miles down the road at the village of Arpaia, they joined the main road heading southwest to Naples.

That evening they slept on, near, and around the cart at the port of Naples. The next morning, Wednesday, March 28, 1883, the boys feasted on the hard brown bread and wine their parents had packed. Zi Michele tearfully hugged each boy as they boarded the ship. The old man knew he would never see his son or any of the other boys again. He gave his bread to his son and told him to split it with the other four boys. Four boys from town had recently gone to Argentina. Now his son and four more he had seen grow up were leaving. It seemed to him that Moiano was losing all of it's young.

Zi Michele stood on the dock and waved goodbye as the ship pulled away from the dock. He watched the ship until his poor eyesight could not be sure the boys were still on deck. With tears streaming down his face he got aboard his little cart and headed back home. In the first letter Ferdinando received from his mother he learned that his dad, Zi Michele died one week to the day after they had left Naples for America.

The sea was calm from Naples to Palermo. Many young people from Calabria and Sicily boarded the same little ship there. Several days later, when the ship entered the Atlantic, it sailed into a spring storm. This ended any merriment. Nearly all of them would suffer from seasickness for the balance of the voyage.

Steerage in those old ships was a trying experience. Sanitary conditions did not exist and the odor was overwhelming. Fresh water was only available on the ship's deck.

The diet, for those who had an appetite, consisted of salted fish, salted pork, and salted meat from an unknown specie of animal. These three foods, in the same order, were repeated for the entire trip.

Ferdinando carried the instructions from the young man from Arpaia in his wallet. The instructions included directions from lower

Manhattan to a railroad station and then to Albany, New York. Fate however, stepped in to change all their plans. After the first night on the ship, Ferdinando's shoes and wallet containing the instructions were stolen. The boys remembered only the name for their sponsor, Giovanni DeAngelo, and the city of Albany, and that a railroad would take them there. For the remainder of the journey everyone slept with their shoes on and their meager funds pinned under their clothes.

Antonio, the oldest of the group, did not get seasick, so he took care of the other boys. He got them fresh water when they asked for it and the rest of the time he looked for a pair of shoes for Ferdinando. He was able to find two left shoes of different sizes. The left shoe fit Ferdinando quite well but the shoe on his right foot was considerably larger than his foot.

As their ship neared New York harbor the young men went on deck to enjoy the fresh air and all the harbor traffic. None of them paid any attention as they sailed by two small islands. One was Ellis the other was Bedloe.

The government chose Ellis Island to be an immigration processing station in 1884. It went into full service in 1892. After 1886, the Statue of Liberty on Bedloe Island garnered the attention of everyone arriving in New York.

Eighty-nine passengers, including the five sick and weak young men from Moiano, were on deck waiting to disembark. Promptly at 6:30 a.m., on the 42nd day of the trip, the ship docked in Pier 18 in New York City.

As the passengers walked across the gangplank to the pier they could see rats scurry across the wooden support braces beneath them. In the still water there was debris and dead vermin.

The immigrants were all lead to a small barge for their trip to Castle Gardens. Breathing the fresh air, away from the stench of excrement and vomit they had lived with on the ship, was invigorating to everyone.

The barge hugged the Manhattan coastline heading south. It provided small glimpses of each New York City east-west street. The new arrivals could see much traffic, every conceivable wagon, large and small, loaded with commerce of the day, pulled by horses. Many buildings were larger than any they saw in Naples or Palermo, plus New York City never seemed to end.

Soon the barge pulled up to another dock. A big round concrete fortress, Castle Garden, faced them. Castle Garden was where immigrants were processed before completion of the Ellis Island facility. It was located 35-feet offshore on the southern tip of Manhattan Island, and started its life as the southwest Battery in 1811. Later the fort became Castle Clinton in honor of DeWitt Clinton, a former mayor of New York City and later governor of New York State. In 1824 Castle Clinton was ceded to New York City.

On August 3, 1855, Castle Garden, under lease to the State of New York, opened as an immigrant-landing depot. A short time before it opened, Castle Garden was joined to the mainland by fill dirt. From 1855 to 1889, more than eight million immigrants, two out of three persons immigrating to the United States, came through the Castle Garden building. Over the period from 1855 to 1953, it was an important stop for all arriving immigrants. First, as an immigration station, then when the Ellis Island facility opened the immigrants were taken by boat to Castle Gardens. It became more commonly known, and referred to as The Battery.

After 1883, as the number of immigrants gradually increased, more buildings were erected outside the Garden. Brick walls replaced the wooden fences. In December of 1891, the last immigrants went through Castle Garden. The new center opened on Ellis Island on January 1, 1892. Ellis would become a place of great happiness for immigrants who passed all the inspections and were allowed to find their place in America and despair for a few persons who did not pass inspection and were sent back to their country of origin. The Italians who I knew talked warmly of their experiences at that facility. However, for some Italians it would later become a prison. During World War Two, it became just that for many Italian nationals and immigrants who had not received their citizenship papers. This is another story and will be told in a later chapter.

The immigration station at Castle Garden was extra busy and the boys spent most of the day in one line or another. Since none of the five from Moiano had passports, or any other travel papers, a paper tag was pinned on each individual, which read "WOP" (without papers). Each processor at Castle Garden knew this fact, which helped them to process shiploads of these new immigrants. The boys told the processors their sponsor was Giovanni DeAngelo, whom they did not know, and Albany their destination, of which they had little knowledge.

Those released earlier in the day waited for the last person to join them. At another pier down the street from the station a small barge was anchored. Luckily, none from Moiano ended up there. This barge, headed for Staten Island at the end of the day. A quarantine hospital located there was for the immigrants who were sick or did not pass the medical examination in Castle Garden. Most of them were placed on another ship and returned to their homeland. U. S. Law required the steamship lines to provide free return passage for these individuals.

At three o'clock that afternoon the last one joined the group. Without the written instructions they had no idea what they would now do. Each hoped that someone else in the group would have a good idea.

After leaving the Castle Garden building, the boys were in a crowd of other immigrants. Individuals solicited them to exchange money; others sold small bags of food for 50¢. As hungry as they were they could not afford that much money for one paper bag that contained a small salami sandwich and a banana.

Antonio, approaching any individual who he thought might answer a question, said Albany, hoping to get a response in Italian. Soon the other four were asking the same question. Nobody seemed to understand or respond.

A stranger, who spoke Italian, but dressed in American style clothes, told Antonio to wait, and he would return to help him. Even though the other boys noticed Antonio was no longer asking for directions, they continued because they did not know what they would do if they failed to find their way to Albany.

Soon the man who spoke Italian returned to Antonio. The other four boys noticed Antonio obviously in deep conversation with him. Each found their way through the crowd to where Antonio and the stranger were standing. Speaking in Italian he told Antonio that work was scarce in Albany, which was not true. However, he said that the New York Lake Erie and Western Railroad (Erie Railway) needed workers and jobs were available.

The New York Lake Erie and Western Railroad, completed in 1851, spanned 469 miles from Piermont on the Hudson, to Dunkirk on Lake Erie. At the time it was the longest railroad in the World. It was also the widest, in that its rails were six feet apart. Every other railroad being planned and built in America, had rails that were four feet eight and a half inches apart. This gauge is still used today. Along with being the longest and widest, it would also probably be the poorest. Those who came to work for the line found much adversity.

Railroad steam engines during this period began to use soft coal instead of wood. At the ash pit, ashes were removed from the steam engines before repairs could be done. Removing the wood ashes, which quickly burned out and only ashes remained, was easy. Removing the soft coal ashes, which burns much longer, was something else. The burning soft coal fused, making clinkers. The clinkers had to be broken with iron rods so they could pass through the grates under the firebox. The men doing this work were so close to the open engine firebox they continually were breathing in the soft coal gases. They soon developed breathing problems with persistent coughing. Because the individuals who worked at the ash pits wouldn't work there any longer, the Erie and other railroads solicited arriving immigrants to fill those positions.

Chapter
2 *Finding work in America*

Each boy strained to hear the conversation between the Italian-American and Antonio. They realized this stranger was offering Antonio a job. The anticipation of possible work was overwhelming. Antonio said he had four other friends. They all smiled when the Erie representative said there are jobs for everyone. They continued listening with broad smiles as this man sent from heaven explained about the work and pay.

He walked with the immigrants to the overhead rail line, a short walk from the Castle Gardens building. Their smiles widened when he remarked that meals were free until they got to their final destination. He placed them on the train going uptown and told them to get off at Chamber Street. He gave Antonio directions, written in Italian, to the Erie terminal in Jersey City.

At Chamber Street, they walked several blocks to the pier on the Hudson River and boarded the ferry, which had a sign on its smoke stack that read "Erie Railway." On the way across the Hudson River none of the boys looked back at New York City. All looked ahead at what little they could see of their destination.

Above the dock, where the ferry stopped, a sign read "New York Lake Erie and Western Railroad," at the other end of the board walk, was another sign, "Erie Railway passenger terminal." The terminal was always very busy with people rushing off and on the incoming and outgoing trains. The Erie representative in Jersey City, New Jersey, recognized them as immigrants sent from Castle Gardens. He greeted them in Italian and explained how prosperous they would be with the money they could earn, and that many other Italians chose to work for the Erie.

At an office next to the waiting room, each man signed a work application in Italian. The representative then took them to the station's cafeteria, where the day's menu included all of the spaghetti and tomato sauce with meat, and lettuce salad that they could eat. The boys could not remember when, in their young lives, their hunger had been so completely satisfied.

They spent the night in the station bunkroom with 35 other Italians who had arrived on the same ship. All the Italians expressed, each in his way, his thanks to God for guiding them as He had. With their hunger more than satisfied, everyone slept well.

The next morning at 7:00 they ate breakfast in the cafeteria. The menu consisted of very salty ham, eggs, and pancakes. They ate as many eggs and as much ham they thought the company would allow.

After breakfast they all boarded Number One, the Westbound Day Express, scheduled to leave at 9:15 a.m. The train consisted of one baggage-mail car, three coaches, a dining car, a sleeping car and a coach for immigrants at the end. The wooden coach was old and dilapidated. Built for the line 40 years before, it had recently been converted to run on the Erie's new standard gauge rail. The interior had hard wooden benches and there was no drinking water or toilets. The locked Pullman car ahead of the coach confined the Italians to this car.

The five from Moiano had tickets to the American village of Susquehanna Depot, Pennsylvania. The group from Abruzzi and Sicily tickets read Hornellsville, those from Calabria went to Buffalo and Meadville.

A story of Slavic immigrants in the early part of the 20th century is interesting. Contents of letters from America, advised those who planned on going to America, that Endicott Johnson (EJ) would surely hire them. Word generally got around to friends, relatives, and strangers, that when they arrived in America, they needed to simply ask for directions. Not knowing the language, the immigrant learned that two words "Where EJ?" were sufficient.

By this time the immigration station at Ellis Island was in full service. At the Ellis Island Railroad office, when the immigrants asked the clerk "Where EJ?" the clerk would sell them a ticket to Binghamton, New York. It also included written instruction on how to get to the Erie station in Jersey City.

Other immigrants had written instructions, sent from America, on how to get from Ellis to the Erie in Jersey City. After leaving Ellis Island, the immigrant went by ferry at the foot of Manhattan, disembarking at The Battery.

To be assured, the immigrant might ask "Where EJ?" The person answering would point at the overhead rail line and say, "get off at Chamber Street." At Chamber Street one followed everyone else and boarded the ferry for Jersey City. At the Jersey City Erie station ticket window, if the immigrant had not bought a ticket at Ellis Island, he asked "Where EJ?" The ticket agent would reach in the ticket rack and pull out a ticket for Binghamton, NY.

On arriving in Binghamton it was easy for the immigrant to find the Endicott Johnson shoe factories. For this reason, the great majority of Endicott Johnson employees, in the early part of the 20th century, were from the Slavic countries of Poland and Czechoslovakia.

The Day Express began moving with a jolt and it ran slowly for quite a while through a maze of rail lines like spider webs, passing other rail traffic coming east. As the webs of rails were left behind, the train picked up more speed.

The sky became darker and it began to rain. All on the passenger car were dry and comfortable. For a couple of hours there was much talk among them, each comparing his life and home in Italy. They found the reasons they all came to America were similar. There was excitement in their voices when they spoke of the stated hourly pay of 10¢, buona paga (good pay) they all agreed.

The station names included Passaic, Patterson, Turners, as the rain continued. Just before arriving in Port Jervis the rain had stopped and the sun was shining. The train slowed while passing a track gang aligning the rails. Someone in the track gang realized that fellow Italians were in the last coach shouted "Paisano, Paisano," windows quickly opened, and all waved back shouting "Paisano."

Each person now realized that his life had changed. Thoughts of their families made them sad and for the first time they began to miss their homes in Italy. They silently sat looking out the train windows at the strange land filled with mountains and forests.

The train snaked alongside the Delaware River. With windows left open the noisy creaking of the wooden coach and the rhythmical snapping of the train wheels on the rail joints made it hard to carry on any conversation. Occasionally the engine whistle sounded. When the wind was right, smoke from the engine came in the open windows and some of them got soot in their eyes.

Each community had a small station and a few homes scattered in the forest. People stopped what they were doing to wave at the train. The names printed on the stations read Lackawaxen, Narrowsburg, Cochecton, Callicoon, and Lordville. All of these small hamlets looked alike.

This group was lucky they were on a "through train" and would reach their destination in just a few hours. The Erie, and all the other eastern railroads, ran trains for immigrants only. These trains had no priority on the rail lines. The equipment was the oldest the lines had, and much of it, like the coach they rode, had no drinking water or toilet facilities. The immigrant trains went from one railroad siding to another to get out of the way of regular passenger and freight traffic. A trip from New York to Chicago could take as long as three days to complete.

The Erie Railway timetable of May 14, 1855, listed an immigrant train. Scheduled to leave New York at 6:00 p.m., it arrived in Dunkirk at 5:23 the second morning. In comparison the Night Express scheduled from New York at 5:30 p.m. arrived in Dunkirk at 12:00 noon the next day.

Soon after the train left Lordville it slowed to a crawl. Just ahead a boxcar on a westbound freight had a problem and needed to be removed from the train. The defective freight car was switched in the siding. The train then had to back slowly in the same siding to get out of the passenger train's way.

Because they had eaten so much ham that morning, the Italians were very thirsty. Ferdinando was taller than anyone else at 5 foot 11 inches, and the thinnest at barely 130 pounds. He was also the joker of the group. He seized the opportunity seeing the river just a few steps down the bank from the train. He jumped off the slowly moving train, skipped over the eastbound track, then lost his balance and slipped down the bank and fell in the river.

The other Italians laughed loudly as he paused for a moment neck deep in the water with one shoe held up out of the water. This was funny to everyone except Ferdinando. He had to sit with wet clothes in that drafty train two more hours. When the train came to a complete stop the rest of the boys carefully ran down to the river to get a drink of water. The train began moving again passing the siding as the crew of the freight watched.

The train slowly continued then stopped at a new station identical to all the others made of wood clapboard. From their passenger car the Italians could see two huge windows at the east end of the new station. Just above and between the windows a worker was on a ladder. He struggled by himself holding the new station sign (Hancock), while trying to drive a nail to secure the sign to the station building.

Way behind, and west of the station, they could see a big log wagon being unloaded at the sawmill. As the train slowly headed west, they saw another big wagon, pulled by four horses, with a load of logs heading for the same sawmill. They realized that Americans used horses, which is why they had not seen a ciuccio all day.

The next stop was Deposit, New York. Two large pusher engines were in the siding, right next to where their car had stopped. Afraid of these engines so close by, they quickly closed the windows that had been left open. The boys could not know that they soon would be removing hot ashes from these very engines.

After leaving Deposit the train headed southwest and slowed considerably. The engine struggled to pull the seven-car train up the hill to Gulf Summit. There was no river, no houses just the train, mountain and forests. After 30 minutes, at the top of the summit, the train began to pick up speed.

The Moiano boys practiced pronouncing the name of the town printed on their passes (Susquehanna Depot). They considered themselves lucky that they would arrive at 4:00 p.m. The group going to Hornell had another 4-hour trip; the Buffalo group, 8 hours and Meadville group even longer with a wait in Hornell for a connecting train.

As the train crossed the Starrucca Viaduct they looked down at the small hamlet of Lanesboro. Then, ahead and below, they could see many homes scattered in the forest and a much larger river, the Susquehanna, swollen this time of year because of the spring rains.

Susquehanna Depot was located on the south side of the Susquehanna River. It later dropped "depot" from its name. The station, shops, westbound yards, and the half-mile of Susquehanna Main Street are flat. Otherwise, when walking from one part of town to another, people walked up or down a hill.

The boys were excited as they waited to get off the train. Through the train windows they noticed the repair shops with smoke stacks, more tracks and switch engines. Some of the shop workers were outside to watch the Day Express pull into town 35 minutes late.

As the young Italian stepped off the train a man was waiting to get on their coach with a basket full of sandwiches for the remaining Italians. A car inspector seeing them yelled to his fellow worker, "Jesus Christ! There, I told you they were hiring more of those Italian WOPS!" Apart from their dress identifying them as immigrants, at least one of them still had the WOP tag pinned on his shirt.

Susquehanna station, during late afternoon, was the busiest place in town. Several of the local old-timers met there when the weather permitted. The meeting place was on benches in front of the waiting room. Three passenger trains coming through town in three hours provided much entertainment, as they noted who was coming into and leaving town.

The brick passenger station impressed the new arrivals. In the station restaurant they had their last free meal, each was given a plate with a salami sandwich and mashed potatoes. Because they were hungry they wolfed down their sandwiches. The American white bread stuck to their palates. Identifying the unfamiliar mashed potatoes only by the odor, they all chuckled at the same time but none ventured to eat them.

The passenger train quickly departed. An eastbound freight came roaring by the station with two engines in front, belching steam and black smoke with two pusher engines on the train's rear belching even more steam and black smoke. Day and night these eastbound trains could be heard on West Hill, Main, West Main, and Washington Streets, and later on, even up on Prospect Street.

When the men finished eating, another man approached them. His face and hands were almost black from the residue of soft coal dust. They all smiled when he addressed them in Italian, "Buon giorno Paesani." He told them he worked in the ash pit, where they would work. His name was Pietro, he was from Calabria, and was the only one left from his group who had come to Susquehanna four years earlier.

He gave each person an identification card that allowed him to buy food on credit at Lannon and Baxter grocery store on Main Street. He said they must all report at the station at 6:00 the next morning. Because the weather was warm, the station windows were open. They could hear the click clack of the telegraph coming from inside the telegraph office. Pietro led them out of the restaurant, then inside another station door, up the stairs and out the back door, then across the short bridge to a rooming house on Front Street.

Pietro smiled as he left the new arrivals with the landlady. She told them how much the room rent was, and that it was due immediately after receiving their first railroad pay. The Italians, who did not speak English, could only guess what she was saying. She motioned them to follow her out the back door and up a path to the outhouse and opened the door. It was obvious to the Italians what it was used for.

That evening the Italians went to look for Lannon and Baxter Grocery store where they bought enough bread and salami for breakfast. On Saturday evenings, Main Street was very busy. Horses and wagons were weaving back and forth, and many people were visiting with each other. As they gazed into each store they believed everything in the world to buy was displayed in Susquehanna's store windows.

Down at the Bronson Piano store a big freight wagon with two horses was blocking the sidewalk, and most of the street. Three men were trying to slide a piano up a wooden ramp, but it had slipped off the main bed of the wagon. They could not get the piano back down because the end of the piano rested between the ramp and the wagon. The three men, (Mr. Bronson and his customer, plus another man) who attempted to load the piano, were not strong enough to safely move it either way.

The Smith family, four boys and two girls and their mother, wondered if they could help. Bronson was upset; he had agreed to deliver the piano this evening and now was face to face with the prospect of badly damaging the instrument that cost him $40. A man and woman, who were aware of the problem, held the horses in case they became spooked and lurched forward.

Antonio and two of the Italians helped, and between all of them, managed to lift it enough to secure one end on the wagon. The ramp fell to the ground making an exploding noise. To Bronson's relief, they were then easily able to slide it the rest of the way securely on the wagon.

Ferdinando, not one of the Italians helping with the piano, noticed Mrs. Smith as she grabbed her two girls and pulled them behind her. She had heard that in Binghamton, Italians were raping little girls. Although Mrs. Smith never read this in the daily newspaper, *The Binghamton Leader*, she believed the gossip to be true.

The Italians received only a smile from Bronson. They found no acceptance from others in Susquehanna, and later would find even less acceptance at work.

At 6:00 the next morning they met Pietro at the station and he brought them to the ash pit. Antonio and Ferdinando started work right away with Pietro. The other three boys started that evening at 6:00 for the night shift.

It didn't matter to the boys that they had the hardest and dirtiest jobs, performed in terrible weather. They were earning money. The pay, 10¢ an hour, allowed them, if they saved on food, to repay their parents in less than ten weeks. Ten weeks later they had saved enough money for their return trip home. Thereafter they accumulated a nest egg for their future in Italy. It was not unusual in this period for a man to have his wallet stuffed with two hundred or more dollars when he returned to Italy.

The nature of the work caused them to have many coughing spells. Some coughed so hard they almost strangled as they tried to bring air into their lungs. Those who could not adjust returned home in less than two years. Antonio, who was physically strong, remained for about five years. He outlived all of his peers, and died in 1936, in his home in Moiano.

Our group from Moiano worked hard and diligently followed instructions. Many of the other workers were unhappy, they worried that the "goddamn wops" were going to take over their jobs.

The Italians found security among themselves. Happiness came when a friend or relative arrived from Italy. Sadness was when one left for home. In Italy, they had a close family circle. In America, the family became even more important.

Ferdinando, the only one who kept everyone laughing, in spite of the hardships at work, developed a constant cough. By October he was not able to work at all. His fellow Italians attended to him during their off-hours. It was not easy when all five shared the same room in the rooming house.

Antonio decided to check with a travel agent. The travel agent advised of a ship leaving for Italy in early November. The men bought a new American overcoat for Ferdinando so he would be warm on the boat. They all sadly bid farewell to their very sick friend.

On the train to New York, Ferdinando hardly seemed alive. Antonio, who accompanied him, became momentarily upset with his new country and proclaimed, "managgia a America" (damn this America). After bringing Ferdinando to the ship the next morning, Antonio wished him well, "Dio vi benedice." Then he sadly returned to Susquehanna.

On the ship Ferdinando spent almost all of his time in his bunk, the cough did not subside, days and nights ran into each other.

The ship arrived at the port of Naples the day before Christmas. The crew helped Ferdinando off the ship. He sat on the dock for a long time to rest because he knew he had a long way to go. He got up and started to walk, but after a few steps, he collapsed. A local fisherman saw how sick he was, and overruled Ferdinando's objections of assistance, then helped him to his own home. That evening, Christmas Eve, the fisherman's wife fed him boiled fish and Italian wine. For the first time in many weeks he slept soundly.

On Christmas morning the fisherman took him to Acerra, a little village just east and north of Naples. There he found a local contadino (peasant) who agreed to take him to Arpaia. At Arpaia a man who had known Ferdinando's dad took him the rest of the way to Moiano.

Ferdinando's mother, already saddened from the loss of her husband, was distraught over her son's condition. She was at his side night and day. Giovanni Palma came over evenings and spent as much time as he could with his critically ill friend. One morning, in late January 1884, terribly weakened from his coughing and persistent fever, and while he sat facing the Italian sun outside the little dwelling where he was born, Ferdinando quietly died.

Meanwhile, also in December, four other boys from Moiano boarded a ship in Naples to go to America. Getting through Castle Garden was easier for this group. It was important that all arriving immigrants have a sponsor (a spouse, or relative or friend) in America, a definite destination, and some promise for work. The boys' sponsor was Antonio Saccone in Susquehanna Depot, and the promise of work on the Erie Railroad.

With the detailed travel instructions, they arrived in Susquehanna, in the middle of January 1884. It was like a holiday when the eight Moiano boys were re-united in America. Each recounted their experiences during their trip to America. All missed Ferdinando and were saddened to know how sick he was when he left America. They all laughed when Antonio told the story of Ferdinando's slide into the river. Two months later there was much sorrow when word came of Ferdinando's death. It was several days before these immigrant Italians were talking and smiling again.

Life in Susquehanna for the immigrants was not easy. In the winter the boarding house was cold. When there was a fire in the downstairs parlor stove, only the landlady's family and a few select boarders were allowed to share the warmth. Not one of the Italians was invited.

On Sunday mornings those not at work went to Mass at St. John's Catholic Church. They stood in the back during the service and left right after Communion. The Irish priest considered them uncouth and somewhat barbaric. Most of the time they did not place anything in the collection basket. When they did, it might be one cent. The priest expected at least one hour's pay from the parishioners. To the Italians the Latin Mass was familiar, but the sermons said in English were not. They did not feel close to this Catholic Church in America

Eventually, all of the boys returned to Moiano. For the rest of their lives, America and Susquehanna became a faded memory of their youth. They married and raised families with some financial security. However, the money they had earned in America did not last long enough to make their children financially secure.

There was always someone from Moiano in Susquehanna who could be a sponsor. For this reason, it was easier for the younger generation to go to Susquehanna. Many of them were children of the original immigrants. Unlike their parents and grandparents, these new arrivals would stay permanently in the United States.

Chapter
3 Back home in Italy

When so many young men left for America, the situation for young women grew worse. With no work available locally and few marriage opportunities, many of them went to Naples to take a job as a housemaid.

This was also true for Maria Meccarillo, my maternal grandmother, born on February 5, 1862. Maria was a tiny woman barely five feet tall, fair skin, with piercing blue eyes and long black hair. In Naples she quickly found work as a housemaid for a large family. Maria liked working as a maid because it was easier than working *coppa monte*. On her first job, an ugly problem she had not anticipated surfaced. Her employer made sexual advances toward her. He promised extra pay if she would cooperate. Three weeks later, after receiving her first pay, she simply left the house.

She inquired at other nearby mansions and the Alessandro family quickly hired her. Signore Alessandro, an exporter of Italian wines and citrus fruits, was quite wealthy. Maria slept in a small cottage on the mansion grounds. She ate her meals with the family and both Signora and Signore Alessandro made no demands other than her assigned work. They occasionally gave her time off to visit her parents in Moiano.

A year and a half later, Italian wines and citrus fruit were in less demand abroad. This greatly reduced the Alessandro's income. They reluctantly had to let Maria go. With an excellent referral from Signore Alessandro, Maria went to work for the Artini family, which included the parents and three boys. The mother was ill and in bed most of the time. Maria slept in a small room on the third floor of the Artini mansion.

It wasn't long before the same ugly problem she encountered on her first job started, but this time it was worse. Both Signore Artini and his eldest son made sexual advances towards her. However, the opportunity for the two males to annoy her decreased considerably, because as Signora's condition became worse, Maria had to spend day and night at her bedside.

Early one morning, four months after Maria arrived, Signora Artini died. Two days later a slow procession of family and friends went to the mausoleum for the burial ritual. That morning Maria wore both of her dresses with her few possessions in the pockets. She accompanied the funeral procession but during the services she once more walked away.

She had no intention of returning to the Artini home or putting herself in the same situation again. Feeling she was a failure as a maid, she cried as she walked home through the lonely curved streets of Naples.

It was late August and it did not get dark until 7:00 p.m. In order to get home before dark she walked at a brisk pace. This walk home was not pleasant as it was when she worked for the Alessandro family. At that time she went home with presents for her parents. This journey home was full of worries; how could she now support herself? What should she do? No answers came to her as she walked. She had no way knowing the answer was already close at hand.

Giovanni Palma's father died three weeks before Maria returned. A small plot of land *coppa monte* was now all his. Because he could support another person thoughts of marriage entered his mind. Maria was the only girl he had ever considered for marriage. After he became courageous enough to speak to her parents (as custom dictated) he learned they didn't know when she would return. They thought she'd be there on September 8, the Moiano Festa (celebration) of the *Madonna Della Libera*, but she returned a week earlier.

Ever since she took her first job in Naples, several men had courted her. Due to her experiences there, she wanted nothing to do with any of them. However, when Giovanni Palma came to see her everything was different. Maria's parents were no problem for Giovanni they knew him as a gentle and hard-working young man. Maria graciously accepted his proposal for marriage. Giovanni Palma and Maria Meccarillo were married the following January in the year of 1885.

The *coppa monte* harvest provided enough food for Giovanni and Maria Palma, and their four children (sons Michele 12, Nicole 7, Filippo 4, and the youngest and only daughter, Maddalena, not quite 2 years old). But as the children got older they required more food than their plot *coppa monte* could produce. For several months Maria and Giovanni discussed the solution. Either the whole family should immigrate to America, or Giovanni should go alone and send for the rest of them later. They agreed he should go first, and then send for them later.

Giovanni had two sponsors, one in Susquehanna and another in New York. Susquehanna was not an option for Giovanni. He remembered Ferdinando and how sick he was when he returned from Susquehanna 16 years ago. He decided to take his cousin's suggestion about New York, because he had written that New York City had numerous job opportunities.

In May of 1899, after being processed at Ellis Island, he took the ferry to The Battery, and before he got off the ferry he spotted his cousin waiting for him. He took Giovanni to the employment office at 80 Mulberry Street (Mulberry Street and the surrounding area became known as Little Italy). In March of 1901, he returned to Italy to see his family. Thirty days later, he boarded another ship and headed back to New York, arriving on May 7, 1901. He got through Ellis Island by the middle of the afternoon. He went back to the employment office where he was directed to return to the same job he had before he left.

Giovanni, his cousin and other men, worked building the tunnels for the new subway. A large steam shovel dug the long trenches required for the subway and the men followed behind the big machine, and did manual chores to prepare the tunnel floor for the cement and rail workers.

New York, Giovanni felt, was a monstrous metropolis. No matter how far he went, he was still in the city. Since his arrival the first time in 1899, he could see many changes. There were many more buildings, and electric lights were on more street corners.

Giovanni stayed in a little room on the third floor, near where his cousin and family lived on Mulberry Street. It was a very small room and it had no electricity. The building was overrun with rats and roaches. He could not keep the roaches away. With the rats he was a little more successful. He kept them out by stuffing rags in several holes in the wall of his room, and each night he wedged a wooden slat under the door to the hall.

The big problem was when he had to go to the bathroom down the hall. He would see rats scurrying through the holes behind the toilet. He spent as little time there as needed.

He bought his food in a delicatessen down the street. Most of the time he had eaten it before he returned to his room. Occasionally his cousin invited him to Sunday dinner. This was practically the only time in America that he sat down at a table to eat.

Once a month he wrote a letter home, which included a bank money order so his family could live comfortably while he was in America. He was happy each time he received a letter from Maria. At the end of each letter the boys wrote "Salute tadi" (Greetings to daddy). He smiled one entire evening and the following day, when on the end of one letter, along with the boys little note, in a small child's scrawl was "Mio tadi, Maddalena."

Giovanni's cousin and many of the other Italians he worked with had come to America with their families. Those who had come over alone later sent steamship tickets home for their wives and children to join them.

Giovanni decided against remaining in America because on cold and damp days, during fall, winter and spring, pain in his joints made him uncomfortable. As the months went by the arthritis became worse and his will to ignore the pain weakened. He began to count the days when he could pack up and return to his family and the warm sunshine of Italy.

By the middle of 1904 he had accumulated over $300, which was more than he had the first two years. The Palma family was rich. He packed his belongings, bought a present for Maria and each one of his children, and happily boarded a ship for Naples and home. This time he had no plans to ever return to America.

The fall before Giovanni returned, Maria had entered Maddalena in school. She believed Maddalena was too frail to work *coppa monte*, and that an education would be useful for her. After returning to Italy,

Giovanni took Maddalena out of school. He said that she would learn to read and write, then she would write to boyfriends when she got older.

He was right. Maddalena did write to a boyfriend, and many others when she got older. During World War One, many parents in town asked her to read the letters received from sons and husbands who were fighting the Germans, Austrians, and Hungarians. She also wrote the replies to the same sons and husbands.

With some of his fortune earned in America, Giovanni bought additional land *coppa monte* from a family who had immigrated to America. On this land there were two large olive trees that would make dark oil for home consumption and sale.

Maria Palma was an accomplished cook who spent most of her afternoons preparing meals for the family. She wore a big apron that covered her long skirt. She prepared pasta with tomato and meat sauce. Meats prepared for the evening meal included meatballs, fresh pork, prosciutto and beef. Chicken soup with homemade egg noodles was another family favorite. Green vegetables, available for most of the growing season, completed their meals.

Giovanni Palma lived to see his family grow up, and he was present at three of his four children's weddings. Giovanni Palma died of a stroke in 1934.

His wife, Maria Palma, lived until she was 92. Before her death in 1953 she received a visit from Anna, my sister, her American granddaughter, whom she had not seen since 1925, when Anna was 9 months old.

Chapter 4 *The Moiano Mango Family*

Giovanni Mango (who was my father's father) had courted many of the eligible females. Even though Moiano had more women seeking husbands than there were men available, none of them were interested in him. They believed he was cruel and uncouth. Nevertheless, to everyone's surprise, Francesca Oropallo, a very sweet and gentle person, accepted his proposal of marriage.

Her father did not object to Francesca's decision. He thought Giovanni was a serious and hard-working young person and gave his blessing to their marriage.

Giovanni and Francesca Mango had six healthy boys; Angelo was born in 1885, Pietro in 1888, Bernardino in 1892, Pasquale and my father Giuseppe (Peppino), fraternal twins born 1895, and Francesco (Cicco), was born in 1898.

Giovanni preferred his two oldest sons, Angelo (Lillo and Pietro; they received everything, within reason, he could provide. He explained that the older boys would not always be at home and they needed money to go to America. The younger boys received little positive attention from him.

Their mother treated them equally and never scolded them. Father punished them when they did wrong, and at other times, just to vent his anger. They were never sure if they had misbehaved or not. He was especially mean on Sunday evenings after spending all afternoon drinking in the cantina. Francesca walked a fine line between protecting her younger sons, and bringing her spouse's wrath down upon herself. She endured much abuse from him.

The last Mango child, a girl, was born on March 22, 1904. The birth did not bode well for either Francesca or the child. Even though Giovanni knew this, he only sent 8 1/2 year-old Peppino to the midwife's residence to escort Francesca and the baby home. Peppino did all he could to help his weakened mother while she struggled to carry the baby.

Years later he remembered that his mother could only take a couple of steps and then had to ask him to stop for her to rest. It took them a long time to walk the short distance from the midwife's residence to their home.

The boys knew something was wrong because their mother remained in bed. She attempted as best she could to nurse the baby and occasionally she reached out to touch her boys. As she lay near death she prayed to God and Moiano's *Madonna Della Libera (Our Lady of Freedom)* to make her and the new baby well. She cried silently as she asked the Madonna to look over her boys, should God take her now.

The Catholic Church said that our Lady of Lourdes, and our Lady of Fatima, apparitions are well documented. However the apparition of the Madonna Della Libera dates back to the period between the years 1500 to 1600, and few written or verbal accounts of Her have survived. However, many miracles have been attributed to Her over the years. Pope Innocenzo XII first venerated her in 1698.

Statues of the Madonna are in Moiano's two churches, and a picture or small statue of her adorns a prominent place in all Moiano's homes. The celebration on September 8 for the Madonna is the most festive of the year. Many former towns' people come back to Moiano on Her day.

If your immigrant parents were from Moiano, the Madonna Della Libera was a big part of their religious lives. Our parents and all others who migrated from Moiano let us know how important She was. I remember my mother and dad telling us kids of Her before I was three years old. We knew of God first and a very close second was Santa Maria Della Libera. Mother suggested that the Madonna had appeared to several Moiano children coppa monte, centuries before her time.

Sketchy details of one Madonna miracle happened during World War One. One evening a brigade of soldiers, composed of young men from Moiano, made an unchallenged advance through the German-Austrian lines. The men released a pigeon to notify the company commander that they had taken new ground and of their position. The Kaisers Army, having apparently spotted their position closed the hole they had advanced through and there began a murderous crossfire. Hopelessly surrounded and pinned down, they raised their heads only briefly to fire at the Austro-German positions. During a lull in the battle, some in the group and soon the entire soon brigade began praying to the Madonna.

Very slowly, the armies that surrounded them were firing only sporadically. After an hour of prayer, all the shooting had stopped. Very slowly, the brigade that had sustained no casualties was successful in retreating back to the main Italian line. The members of that brigade called it a Madonna miracle.

Francesca's mother was at her side continually. Late in the day of March 25, 1904, the infant child died. Three hours later Francesca, still praying to the Madonna for her boys, died peacefully.

The loss of their mother was catastrophic for the younger boys. The oldest son Lillo had left for America the year before. Shortly after his mother's death, Pietro the next oldest son, left for America to join his brother.

Giovanni was left to raise his four younger boys alone. Although he considered remarriage he didn't believe he had anything to offer another woman except hard work and a ready-made family.

Giovanni's routine of spending Sunday afternoons at the cantina, an expense unjustified when his wife was alive, was not changed by her death. All at the cantina knew he could not stop with one drink. He drank until it closed late in the afternoon. When drunk he looked for ways to vent his violent temper.

One Sunday evening, when he returned home from the cantina, he found just the right trigger to release his anger. The boys had been so busy playing they forgot to add water to the beans cooking on the fire. The beans had burned and were not edible. He vented his wrath on the boys and beat them soundly.

After that, Bernardino, who was 12 years old, assumed the responsibility of looking after his younger brothers and watching the beans on Sundays. During the week, Bernardino stayed home until noon to tend the cooking beans. The rest of the family went *coppa monte* to work.

When Giovanni realized he was leaving his most productive son at home, he decided to have Bernardino work in the field and have one of the twins stay home to watch over the pot of beans.

Peppino was proud his father asked him to look after the cooking of the beans. When his father and brothers left he went outside to check the beans on the fire, to be sure that they had enough water and to keep the fire going. Although the beans did not appear to need water, he added some anyway. At the same time he noticed that the water bucket was nearly empty.

Because he was hungry, he went into the house and opened the breadbox for a piece of bread. He counted 5 slices, one for each member of his family for dinner. His father had taken enough bread for himself and the other boys, but did not leave any for Peppino. His first thought was to eat his piece of bread. But he knew then he would not have bread for supper.

The box his mother used to store dried figs was empty. He remembered that a fig tree just up the hill from his home might provide a good breakfast. He went up the rocky slope on the same path his father and brothers took for *coppa monte*. He fell a couple of times because he had to leave the path to reach the tree. When he got to the tree he had a problem. The figs were too high for him to reach.

Peppino remembered much happier times when his mother would lift and place he and his brothers on a branch of the tree. They would then sit there and eat all the figs they wanted. Try as he might, he could not get enough of a foothold to climb the tree. He noticed a branch that seemed low enough if he went a little farther up the rocky slope.

After much effort he managed to grab a branch from the ground but sadly found the figs were not ripe. Nevertheless, he ate as many of the hard green figs that he could pick.

On his way back home he remembered of the days his mother baked bread. When it was ready, they would sit around the table to eat big slices of hot bread. He also remembered when she cooked polenta. Each boy helped her grind the corn. She would then cook it and oh, how good it tasted.

When he got home he attempted to grind some corn, he did not make the same progress his mother did. The job was too hard for him.

In the meantime the fire under the beans was getting low, so he went outside and added more wood. He also remembered he needed to get water. He emptied the bucket in the clay bowl in the pigpen and then headed for the town square where the well was located. Not long ago he and his brothers, Pasquale and Cicco, accompanied their mother to get the bucket of water. Mother balanced the full water bucket on her head to carry it home from the well.

There were two women at the well who filled the bucket for him, and questioned if he could carry it home. They asked, "Dov'è il vostro fratello piu vecchio?" (Where is your older brother)? Peppino proudly announced, "Sono io che oggi guardo la casa" (I am taking care of the house today).

He did not notice the sad look on their faces. They had seen his swollen left ear and the black and blue marks on the side of his neck where his dad had slapped him the night before. If he could understand why his dad had hit him, he would never do that again, and maybe his dad would not hit him again. He felt sorry for his brother Pasquale who would complain, dad would merely hit him even harder.

Carrying the bucket was more difficult than he thought. His head and his left shoulder hurt. He dragged the bucket most of the way without spilling very much. He thought his dad would be pleased to find it full of water. As he added more wood to the fire under the beans, a sharp pain in his stomach replaced any hunger he may have had.

He prayed "Per piacere Dio se Peppino e davvero buono, forse mamma puo tornare per un po tempo?" "Please God, if Peppino is real good can mother return just for a little bit?" Mother always had something for he and his brothers to eat when they were hungry. She also knew what to give him for a stomachache. She used to tell him to lie down on the kitchen bench when he did not feel good. He did so and quickly fell asleep and dreamed about his mother.

In his dream his mother called "Bernardino, Pasquale, Peppino, Cicco, venite dentro e aiutate mamma con il gradigno" (come in help mother with the corn). She had the rock grinder in the kitchen ready to grind the corn. They each wanted to be first to help. As always, in the end, she resumed the grinding chore. When the bread was done she served each boy a hot piece of bread, some polenta, and a mixture of water with wine. After finishing their little lunch, they went out to play.

A little later, they could smell prosciutto, and when they ran inside, mother gave them each a small sample. She said, "Today is Peppino and Pasquale's birthday. We will have prosciutto and pasta for dinner."

When he awoke, he could still hear his mother's soft voice calling, "Peppino, Peppino." He rubbed his eyes and looked around. Could mother be here? He looked in the little bedroom, walked around their little stone hut, then behind the pigpen. Finally he realized it was just a dream. It did not bother him that the fire under the beans was almost out, because the sun was lower in the sky. He knew dad and his brothers would return soon.

By the time they returned, his stomachache was gone and he felt better. Peppino looked forward to eating his piece of bread and beans. He was expecting approval and a smile on his dad's face when he saw the bucket so full of water.

There was one important chore he had forgotten all day, which was to add water to the beans. They had partially dried and only half of them, in the center of the pot, were edible. Peppino could not understand what his father said as he slapped him across the head. He did hear him say he would fix the "Ti aggiustero domani piccolo figlio di putana" (little son of a bitch tomorrow)!

Even though he was no longer hungry, Peppino ate the two spoonfuls of beans given to him by his dad. He cried softly the rest of the evening. "If only mama was here, she would fix everything." He fell asleep crying.

The next morning Peppino found out how his father would punish him. He made him wear a mohair shirt with no undershirt. The shirt pinched and scratched his back and chest. He wanted to cry but he knew if he did not cry his father would leave him alone. He worked all day in the heat of the Italian sun. As the day progressed the pain became worse. When the wind blew he felt cooler but he could feel blood running down his back and chest.

As he walked home that evening the pain increased. At home Bernardino helped Peppino remove the mohair shirt. The pain was so intense Peppino began to cry. His father, who did not like this, slapped him. Bernardino, who began to cry when he saw his younger brother's chest full of scratches and blood, tried to shield his suffering brother and thus received the wrath of his father's anger.

Pasquale, petrified with fear and not knowing what to do, was spooning some beans out of the pot. His father swung the back of his hand hitting Pasquale across the ear and left an indentation of the wooden spoon across his cheek. Little Cicco, scared to death, ran away.

Maria Oropallo, the boy's aunt, had talked to the women who were at the well yesterday. She was concerned about the situation in the Mango home. She had decided to visit them and walked in at that precise moment. She found three boys crying, Cicco missing, and Giovanni calmly eating beans and bread.

When she saw Peppino, she turned to Giovanni and shouted, "Brutto porco di uomo come puoi maltrattare il tuo proprio figlio in quella maniera!" (Homely pig of a man, how could you mistreat your son in this way)? The old man continued to eat his beans and bread and said nothing.

Peppino began to cry uncontrollably as she gently cleaned him and wrapped a soft cloth around his chest and back. She put olive oil on both he and Pasquale's face and neck, and the black eye developing on Bernardino. She told the old man that she was taking the boys to live in her home.

Uncle Angelo, unhappy and upset when he saw the scared look on all the boys' faces, began to joke with them. The boys' aunt quickly prepared a meal. Angelo sent his son, Francesco, to look for Cicco.

Later that evening, when the three boys were in bed and Francesco still had not returned, Angelo went to look for his son and Cicco. Aunt Maria did not sleep all night because they had not come home yet. She smiled when she saw Angelo, Francesco, and Cicco coming down the road at 6 o'clock in the morning.

Uncle Angelo, who stayed home to calm the boys, played bocce with them. (Bocce is a game played outside with round stones a little larger than a baseball). He told the boys that he would beat them. Each game he would be winning, but near the end, he would do something stupid to lose. The boys laughed at being able to beat their uncle at bocce.

Feeling better that afternoon, Peppino came out to try his hand at beating his uncle. Miraculously, even though he was way behind for most of the game, Angelo made a couple of bad throws, and Peppino won. He laughed for the first time since his mother died.

The next morning, Maria told Angelo that Peppino was eyeing the accordion on the shelf in their little kitchen. Angelo had received it as a present from a friend he had known in America. He told his wife "Lascia giocare l'organetto, lui puo suonarla, nessuno lo sa usare." (Let him play with it, none of us know how to play it).

Angelo took the accordion down and laid it on the table. Being allowed to play the instrument excited the boys, but soon it lost its appeal and they went outside to play. Peppino went outside too, but he took the accordion with him.

Later that day, when Angelo returned home from coppa monte, he heard someone playing "*O Sole Mio.*" Angelo was very perplexed and asked his wife where the music was coming from. She replied Peppino has not put down that accordion all day. Angelo looked surprised and went outside and asked Peppino "Mascalzone chi ti ha insegnato a suonare l'organetto?" (Little son of a gun, who taught you how to play the accordion)?

From that day on, the accordion belonged to Peppino. He entertained anyone willing to listen. He quickly learned to play all the songs he knew. During the celebration of *Madonna Della Libera*, Peppino played his accordion in the parade, for which he received many compliments.

The following week the boys went *coppa monte* with their father but returned to Uncle Angelo's at night. They remained in their uncle's home until he thought it was safe to return home.

It was not long before both Lillo and Pietro sent money home, which slightly improved life for the Mango family. Three days each week, pasta instead of beans was the evening meal. Aglio e olio (garlic and oil) was the usual condiment for the pasta. Other evenings, dinner might be pasta e fasul (pasta and beans). Occasionally, when invited, the boys ate even better at their cousin Mango or Oropallo homes.

Giovanni Mango mellowed as he got older and his boys reached manhood. As he smoked cigars and reviewed his life, I am sure he thought about his relationship with the younger boys. If he could have, I am sure he would like to have returned to the time when they were young. He would change his attitude, and express love for his boys, instead of always being miserable because of his situation.

The twins Pasquale and Peppino turned out quite differently. Peppino was more submissive, and received less beating at the hands of his father. Pasquale was more arrogant and could not understand such treatment. Because he objected while being hit, he received more than his share of beatings.

I am proud of my father, Giuseppe, and my uncles, Pasquale and Bernardino, all of whom I knew well because they stayed in the United States. They did not become alcoholics and abusers. All married and had fine families.

The Mango boys could not wait until they were 16, because this was the age when they could join their older brothers in the United States. The older brothers sent money home so the younger ones could follow. In 1908 Bernardino, almost 16, bought a ticket to America with the money Lillo had sent him. He booked passage on an old, dilapidated ship, which docked in Philadelphia 31 days later.

Bernardino did not care that the passage was rough. He had the freedom to do whatever he pleased. He no longer had to worry about his father's unreasonable anger.

Bernardino disembarked the ship in early May of 1908, and was led to the big immigration building. He cleared it quickly and was soon by himself on the street. Lillo had promised to meet him on the arrival of the ship, but he was not there.

Bernardino walked down the street to a grocery store. Although he could not speak English, he managed to buy a loaf of bread and some salami. Unconcerned, he sat on the curb to wait for his brother. He felt good to be on solid ground again and enjoyed his feast of bread and salami.

Lillo, who had never gone to Philadelphia, misjudged the length of time it would take to go from the train station to the docks. He arrived two hours late. He found his brother sitting on the curb eating bread and salami. Lillo shouted, "Guaglio cosa fai?" (Fellow, what are you doing)?

How mature his brother had become surprised Lillo. The Erie put Bernardino to work at the ash pit. The three Mango boys stayed together in the same rooming house on Front Street.

Before Lillo left for America in 1903, Antonio Saccone had given him detailed instructions on how to get to Susquehanna. When he arrived in Susquehanna, he had a message for Fiore Oropallo from his wife. Fiore had left Italy several months before and had not written home. All Lillo could learn was that Fiore had arrived in Susquehanna, then five or six weeks later he was gone; the assumption was he had returned to Italy.

However, when Fiore arrived the Erie was not hiring. He became tired of the few odd jobs he managed to find. One day he hopped a westbound freight train. With no money, food, or water, he rode in an empty gondola car for five hours before the train stopped in Hornell, New York. When he got off the train, Italian countrymen working in the yards gave him food and water. They advised him that the Erie was not hiring in Hornell either, so he headed west on another freight.

After changing freight trains three times, and on the seventh day, hungry, thirsty, dirty, and tired, he needed to rest from all the riding in freight cars. He got off the freight when it stopped, and found he was in the Cincinnati, Ohio railroad yards. Having seen enough of railroads, he decided to walk away from them.

He walked through Cincinnati and because he didn't have money, he had to beg for food. The Ohio River was his salvation, and fortunately it was a warm day. He spent a couple of hours in the water, clothes and all, until he was clean. Then he rested another two or three hours until he was dry.

With the little English he had learned, he discovered work was available in the Kentucky coalmines. After a few days of walking and riding hay wagons he arrived in Florence, Kentucky and decided to look for work there. We do not know if he ever did work in a coal mine. We do know that he met and lived with a Kentucky teacher. She completely Americanized him; she taught him to speak English, with a Kentucky accent, completely losing his Italian accent.

This relationship lasted until he became terminally ill in 1928. His doctor told him he had only weeks to live. Fiore thoughtfully reviewed the past 25 years. He considered how fortunate he had been to have a woman take care of him. He realized all the hurt he had caused his wife and little children whom he had left destitute in Italy 26 years ago. He tearfully told his distraught common-law spouse that he must seek some forgiveness from his real family before he died. He left Kentucky to seek forgiveness in Italy.

Pietro Mango joined his brother, Lillo, in 1904. Salvatore Mauro had also arrived that same year. A year later Salvatore sent money home so his wife, Francesca, (dad's first cousin) and three month-old son, Mickey to join him. Both Salvatore (Zi Toro) and Francesca (Zi Cesca), were a positive influence for our family when we were children. Soon many Italians from Moiano arrived in America.

During this period there were Italians who came from Giuliano. Giuliano is in the Provincia Di Latine, near Rome. We do not know who was the first to arrive in Susquehanna from Giuliano. We suspect it may have been Giuseppe Radicchi and his father in about 1904. Many from this village followed others, and together they would swell Susquehanna's Italian community.

After Giuseppe Radicchi arrived, he received a letter from home. It advised him that if he did not return to Italy and serve in the Italian army, his brother would have to serve for him. He didn't want his brother to take his place so he returned home. Both he and his brother ended up in the Army.

In 1907, Giuseppe returned to America and joined his father. They opened a very successful shoe store but father and son did not get along well. Then his father opened his own shoe store, he soon tired of America, closed his store, and returned to Italy.

Giuseppe later established a class to teach English to his fellow Italians. The classes were in the evening in his cellar, which opened on ground level of his house on West Main Street. Over the years Giuseppe repaid his fellow Italians for their business. Mother and dad always spoke well of Compare Giuseppe, and Comare Ida Radicchi.

The new arrivals were proud of many fellow Italians who distinguished themselves in America. In 1903, Guglielmo Marconi transmitted the first wireless signal across the ocean. Later on, Rudolph Valentino became a famous movie star. Still later, they would cheer many baseball players who were Italian sons. And they would be proud of the mayor of New York City Fiorello LaGuardia.

By the time the first decade of the Twentieth Century had ended prosperity came to the new American from Italy.

Chapter

5 *More of the second generation comes to America*

In early February of 1912, Lillo Mango returned to Moiano with two large suitcases full of clothes and presents for his wife and brothers. Whenever an older brother returned from America there was much excitement around the Mango home. During this visit he hoped to persuade his wife to return to America with him. As usual, because she wanted to stay close to her mother and father, she would not consider leaving home.

Lillo once more told his younger brothers, Pasquale and Peppino, the pay in America amounted to one lira for each hour of work. Earning the equivalent of 8 Lire (one dollar) each day, would make them rich. Pasquale had decided many months before Lillo returned, that he would immigrate the first chance he got. Giovanni Mango and Raffaele Oropallo, their first cousins, did not hesitate to make the same decision. That first year in America, Giovanni and Pasquale suffered from the cold, and Giovanni may have died were it not for Pasquale. Later Raffaele got in trouble with the law.

Peppino decided not to leave home. He reasoned, since he would be the oldest at home when his brother left, his dad would treat him better. He worried that his dad and little brother Cicco could not do all the work *coppa monte* alone. Besides, he loved his Italian homeland.

On March 27, 1912 Lillo left Italy with brother Pasquale, and their cousin Giovanni Mango, both 16 years old, and cousin Raffaele Oropallo, 17 years old. They boarded the Hamburg America line *S. S. Oceania,* in Naples for America.

Due to the captain's warning of icebergs, the *S. S. Oceania* steamed south of the usual route across the North Atlantic. Nevertheless, passengers could still see icebergs from the port side. It docked in New York on schedule, at noon, Tuesday, April 9, 1912.

The Hamburg-America Line and Italian Lines ships traversing from Naples to New York were much bigger and faster than the ships making the same trek in the 1880s. Steam ships had replaced sailing ships. The galleys of these new ships prepared a wide variety of Italian and American meals.

Lillo was once again seasick. Giovanni and Raffaele spent most of their time in their bunks and ate little. Pasquale had no seasickness and enjoyed every bit of the trip.

In later years Pasquale's son, Chuck, retold this story his father told him. "My dad was extra hungry so he told his brother and cousins that he would go get the noon time lunch for them. The cook put enough macaroni in a tin pail for all four boys.

On the way back he had an idea. Since they ate very little of their food anyway, he told Lillo and his cousins that he had seen the cook sweating and spitting in the macaroni as it cooked. Any hunger his brother and cousins might have had immediately left them. Pasquale then walked away from his brother and cousins, where they couldn't see him, and finished off the pail of macaroni.

A few days after the *S. S. Oceania* left Naples, another ship sailed out of Liverpool, England, on its maiden voyage, expecting to set a speed record to New York. The *RMS Titanic,* the newest and largest ship afloat hit an iceberg at a point four hundred miles southeast of Cape Race on Sunday night April 14. It sank less than three hours later at 2:27 a.m. on Monday, April 15, 1912.

When the boys heard of the Titanic disaster shortly after their arrival in Susquehanna, they remembered seeing icebergs and wondered if they had seen the one the Titanic had hit.

In Susquehanna, Zi Cesca, (Francesca Oropallo Mauro) was proud and excited that her youngest brother, Raffaele Oropallo, had arrived. She decided to have a big dinner for all the new arrivals. At 5:30 Sunday morning she placed a large kettle on the kitchen cook stove, poured two quart-size cans of homemade tomato sauce and two quarts homemade whole tomatoes.

Her husband Salvatore brought up a bucket of coal to add to the wood fire on the kitchen cook stove. Francesca labored for the next hour grinding the meat she bought the day before. She then added spices bread crumbs and eggs to the ground beef, mixed it well and made two dozens meatballs.

She made a braciole with a large piece of round steak. First she sprinkled fresh cut up parsley, oregano, salt and pepper on the meat, then she tightly rolled the steak, as if it was a jellyroll, and tied it with string.

Taking time for church, she tied a scarf under her chin and walked over to St. John's Church for the 7 o'clock Mass. When she returned from Mass an hour later, she browned the meatballs and braciole in a large frying pan before placing them in the simmering tomato sauce.

The rest of the morning she mixed flour and eggs to make egg noodles. Early that afternoon while the meat sauce simmered, she cut the noodles and strung them up to dry. At 6:00 that evening a delicious Italian dinner was ready for all the family and guests.

The Erie Railroad was not hiring so Giovanni and Pasquale went to Albany because they heard that work was available there. Unfortunately they only worked on the New York Central Railroad for three weeks and were laid off. The only other work available was farm work. For the rest of that summer and early fall of 1912, they picked cherries, beans, corn, and apples.

Giovanni was generous with his money. He bought most of the bread and salami they ate that summer and fall. Pasquale accepted his cousin's generosity, and at the same time he added dollar bills to his savings in his wallet.

On the outskirts of Albany, the New York Central Railroad had parked several old boxcars in a siding that was overgrown with weeds. The boys found that the boxcar kept them out of the rain and made fair living quarters.

By late October, the farm work had ended. They had less to eat and by early December, Giovanni had spent all his money. Very cold weather came a week later; temperatures were down to zero at night. The coldest it ever got in Moiano at night in the winter was 32 degrees.

By the end of December both Giovanni and Pasquale became very ill. They closed the boxcar door as best they could and huddled under an old blanket and straw. Neither boy knew when it was Christmas; they were too sick to care.

After being extremely ill for several days Pasquale began to feel better and his thoughts turned to food. He began to scrounge around for firewood. Next he tried to keep a small fire on a piece of iron plating set near the partly open boxcar door. This solved nothing because smoke from the fire filled the boxcar. It caused Giovanni, who was still very sick, much distress.

Each day, as he walked up the street to purchase bread, Pasquale worried about his cousin's condition. One morning Giovanni became delirious; he yelled, cried and appeared to protect himself as if someone was beating him.

Realizing his cousin needed immediate help Pasquale crossed the railroad tracks, headed up the street and began knocking on doors. He yelled, "Mi cugino needa help!" The women at the first four houses slammed the door on him. At the fifth house George Howard, a retired gentleman, recognized Pasquale as one of the boys who used the boxcar for shelter. He went to the boxcar with Pasquale and when he saw Giovanni's condition he told Pasquale to wait until he returned.

He ran back to his house, hitched his horse to the buggy, and headed for the boxcar. He and Pasquale covered Giovanni in a horse blanket, and as Pasquale held him, George Howard snapped the whip and they headed to a nearby hospital. Without money to pay for treatment the hospital turned them away.

They finally found a small hospital on the outskirts of Schenectady that admitted Giovanni. The hospital agreed to get his condition stabilized before releasing him.

Pasquale walked the streets of Schenectady for the next two days. On Front Street, where other Italians lived, he found a room with a potbelly stove and an old dirty mattress on the floor. The savings in his wallet totaled $18. He handed the landlord the first month's rent ($2) and headed back to the hospital.

At the hospital late that afternoon, he rented a taxi (horse and buggy) to take he and his still very sick cousin to their rented room. That evening Pasquale bought chicken soup at a nearby Italian restaurant and returned to the room to spoon-feed his cousin.

Each day people from Front Street, including Pasquale, walked along the railroad tracks with a bucket in search of coal that fell from passing coal trains. One day during a snow storm a coal train stopped. Pasquale was the only one looking for coal. He climbed on a coal car and dumped several buckets of coal on the ground.

Although it continued to snow heavily he knew exactly where the cache of coal was, and was able to carry all the coal to their little room. Because of his scrounging for coal that winter Pasquale was able to keep a fire in the potbelly stove, almost every night.

The restaurant owner who sold Pasquale one bowl of soup each day felt sorry for him and gave him a part-time job washing dishes. He worked during busy hours on Friday and Saturday evenings. His pay was in food. Each day they gave him a large bowl of soup and a loaf of Italian bread.

Slowly Giovanni returned to good health. Pasquale's job and savings kept them in their rented room with meager amounts of food during February, March and April. Giovanni never forgot Pasquale's sacrifice and was grateful to him all his life. He retold the story many times and said if it were not for Pasquale he would have died in that boxcar the winter of 1913.

During the spring and summer of 1913 they once again picked cherries and beans. By October, broke and hungry, Pasquale and Giovanni decided to return to Susquehanna. They knew if they could not find a job, Lillo and Pietro would help them through the next winter.

Chapter

6 *Peppino (Giuseppe) goes to America*

After his brothers and cousins left for America, Peppino had to work longer hours to get the work done. Each day he stayed *coppa monte* after his dad and Cicco returned home. When he finally got home there was never enough food for him to eat. He was doing almost as much work as he and Pasquale used to do together, but all this did not seem to impress his dad.

Peppino listened to two other friends in town who were planning to leave for America in March of 1913. His will to please his father weakened and he decided that when the weather got better in the spring, he would go to America. If his father had asked him to stay in Italy with him, Peppino would have immediately abandoned all plans to go to America.

Giovanni Pepe was very enthusiastic about going to America. He convinced both Carmen Antonio and Peppino to join him. Much of the winter of 1912-1913 was spent planning their trip. Peppino wrote to his brother, Lillo, in November 1912, for an advance of money needed for a one-way ticket.

Lillo remembered that in 1908 the people in Naples sold Bernardino a ticket on a dilapidated old tub that took 31 days to cross the Atlantic and it docked in Philadelphia instead of New York. Furthermore the ship sank on its way back to Naples. Lillo purchased Peppino's ticket and reserved space for all three boys on a good ship scheduled to leave Naples in March of 1913.

Peppino received the steamship ticket in early January. The ship was the Italian Line, *Principe Di Piemonte*, named after the prince of Italy. It steamed from Genoa on March 5, 1913, stopped in Naples on Thursday, March 6, then went directly to New York and arrived on Friday, March 21, 1913.

On Wednesday, March 5, Peppino planned to go *coppa monte* earlier than usual, and awoke at 3:00 in the morning. However it was cloudy and overcast in Moiano, and without the light of the moon, it was so dark he could not see his hand in front of his face. He went back to bed and waited for the first light of the day.

He worked all day until just before dark planting wheat. He stayed too long it was already dark before he got home. The last quarter-mile he had to feel his way down the rocky path.

When he arrived home, day-old beans were the evening fare. He remembered when Pietro left for America years before, and the prior year when Pasquale left, his dad and Lillo had prepared a large pot of pasta, every ones favorite food.

He ate the beans but saved the crust of bread for the next morning. He did not ask, nor did his dad offer him, the crust of bread that he usually would have taken *coppa monte*.

That evening he packed his few belongings. He left out his new trousers, a new shirt and the safety razor his brother had given him last year. He also placed the piece of bread in his cloth bag. Being very tired and still hungry, he went to bed.

The next morning he woke up at 4:00. For the first time he used the safety razor. With only the light of a candle to see with, he cut himself a few times. Because it was cold he wore his *coppa monte* jacket over his new shirt and trousers. Peppino tried to wake his little brother. Cicco, barely awake, held his hand for a moment, waved goodbye and quickly went back to sleep. His dad was not sleeping. He hollered, "Guaglione sta bene, e buon viaggio" (fellow stay well and have a good trip). Very hungry and holding back tears, he walked out into the dark and cold early morning and headed for Carmen Antonio's home where the three boys agreed to meet.

He began to think about his mother, although he had not thought of her for some time. He was sure she would have cooked him a special meal the night before he left, and she would have had extra food packed for him. He knew his mother would have accompanied him to Carmen Antonio's home.

When he rounded the corner on Via Pietroarola he looked across at the darkened house numbered 30. In that house lived Filippo Palma who had decided not to join them on their trip to America. Filippo's sister, Maddalena, was attractive and he liked her a lot. She knew he was leaving for America, but he did not expect her to be awake.

He wiped away tears as he came around the corner. He could see the light of candles that poured through the partially opened front door of Carmen Antonio's home. Giovanni Pepe and his mother and father were already there. Giovanni's father showed very little emotion. Both mothers cried as they kissed their sons. Carmen Antonio's mother handed each boy some food wrapped in three identical white handkerchiefs. Still controlling his tears, Peppino thanked her.

Carmen Antonio's father, Zi Fiore, left for America in 1903, and had never sent money home to his wife and five children. It deeply moved Peppino that Carmen Antonio's family had less to eat than he had, and his mother had prepared food for him!

Repeating the scene just 30 years before when other boys left for America, the boys headed down the road toward Arpaia, while the parents, with tears in their eyes wished them, "Dio vi benedice, scrivi presto." (God bless you and write soon).

The boys were very silent until they were out of town, then hunger began to get the better of Peppino. He unwrapped the white handkerchief and found a very large piece of homemade bread baked with pieces of prosciutto mixed in.

Before the boys reached Arpaia, all three had eaten their prosciutto bread. For the first time in many weeks Peppino had almost satisfied his hunger. He did not eat his own bread and it remained in his bag a long time after he arrived in America.

For the rest of the walk to Naples, Peppino listened to his two friends. While they discussed what they would do with all the money they would earn in America, Peppino worried about the work he should be doing *coppa monte* at this very moment. The boys walked very fast and soon, while the sun ducked in and out of the clouds, they entered Naples.

Just before 10:00, as they neared the bay of Naples, they could see a very large ship being maneuvered to the dock. They knew it was their ship. Clearly painted on its bow was *"Principe Di Piemonte."*

They watched with amazement as men with wives and small children, and many young men like themselves, waited to board the ship. On the ship the boys quickly found the bunks assigned to them in steerage. They could not believe what they saw, beds made with clean white sheets and soft blankets.

Giovanni Pepe toured the ship and found the dining hall. He quickly went back and got Carmen Antonio and Giuseppe (hereafter Peppino is referred to as Giuseppe). All three boys ate a very large dish of spaghetti topped with meatballs. They had already eaten more by noon that day than they had ever eaten on any other day in their young lives. By 4:00 that afternoon the ship was on its way to New York.

The next morning it was after nine when they had to shake Giuseppe awake. On deck that first day, they enjoyed cool ocean breezes, but by the following morning, with Gibraltar just behind them, seasickness set in. Ironically, more food was available than they had ever been offered, but they were not able to enjoy it.

In the early morning of March 21, 1913, feeling better, the boys went on deck when the ship entered New York harbor. The two islands, ignored by the original immigrants from Moiano in 1883, interested this group. Everyone proudly watched as the ship passed the Statue Of Liberty. On the other island (Ellis) they could see a large red brick building.

As the ship headed up the Hudson River the immigrants caught glimpses of each east-west street as the ship slowly made its way to the pier. The view was similar to the one 30 years ago, except that automobiles, busses, and streetcars were seen along with familiar horses and wagons. Taller buildings also changed the skyline of New York. From the ship they were herded to a ferry for their trip to Ellis Island.

At Ellis Island, they walked in single file from the ferry to a very large, cavernous building. All of the different languages they heard, none of which they could understand, both interested and confused them. A man, who barely spoke Italian, asked them for papers, which they did not have. The person next to him had chalk and wrote, as best he could, the letters WOP on their jackets. Not much had changed for Italian immigrants in 30 years.

Doctors listened to their hearts, looked into their mouths, eyes, ears, and hair. They asked, "Town are you from?" (Moiano) "Occupation?" (Farmer) "Who is your sponsor?" (Lillo Mango) "Your final destination?" (Susquehanna). Finally at 2:00 in the afternoon they boarded the ferry that took them to The Battery

Giovanni Pepe could not adjust to America. He returned to Italy less than a year later. Carmen Antonio did adjust, but in 1928 he was dead, leaving a wife and an infant son. The details of his death are in a later chapter.

Lillo and Bernardino boarded the Erie passenger train No 6, at 2:47 a.m. It arrived in Jersey City at 8:15. After they crossed the Hudson on the Chamber Street ferry, they walked over to Mulberry Street (now known as Little Italy). They bought two loaves of bread and a large salami, and then rode the subway to The Battery in lower Manhattan. At The Battery they enjoyed cold ocean breezes while they ate their salami sandwiches. They watched two small boats when they arrived from Ellis Island to unload another group of immigrants. The *William Fletcher* came to unload its passengers, 30 minutes later the *John E. Moore* unloaded some more. Each time either boat docked the boys knew which country most of the immigrants were from by the clothing they wore.

Shortly after 2:00 in the afternoon the *William Fletcher* arrived. Sure enough, a couple of minutes later Giuseppe, Carmen Antonio, and Giovanni came down the walk. Lillo had not written that he and Bernardino would meet them so the boys were not looking for them.

When the boys got off the boat they were especially happy to finally have solid ground under their feet. As they walked toward the El station, Giovanni Pepe read the directions written by Lillo. Being very hungry, Giuseppe paid $1.00 for a small paper bag that contained a banana and a salami sandwich. He broke the sandwich in three equal pieces; each boy quickly devoured his share. Bernardino and Lillo spotted the boys, and watched in amusement as Giuseppe took his first bite of the banana, peel and all.

They let the boys walk by, and then from behind the new arrivals, Lillo shouted, "Contadino di Moiano!" It was a proud moment as all five boys headed for the overhead El station and Chamber Street.

Since they had time before the train left that evening for Susquehanna, they walked over to Mulberry Street. Seeing so many Italians like themselves excited the three newcomers who listened closely as they heard all the different Italian accents. They saw men with pushcarts who sold many kinds of fruits and vegetables, and store windows that displayed groceries and a variety of meats. The boys quickly consumed all the treats bought by Lillo and Bernardino.

They headed back to Chamber Street to board the ferry that took them to Erie Station in Jersey City. Lillo bought a ticket to Susquehanna for each boy. The boys proudly looked at the passes with their brother's name on them, which allowed them to ride without payment.

They arrived in Susquehanna at 12:45 a.m., by now talked out and tired. They all went to the rooming house on Front Street and slept until noon the next day.

When the three boys awoke they sat on the front porch of the rooming house. The rooming house was behind and higher than the station. They could hear the trains, and could see them east of the station. They watched with amazement at the size of the engines, two big ones in front and two more on the rear of each train. When the wind changed directions, smoke and soot enveloped the porch where they were sitting.

Soon Pietro came walking up the dirt road that was Front Street. It was heartwarming for Giuseppe to see his brother, whom he had not seen in three years. He missed his brother Pasquale and cousin Giovanni who were in Schenectady. No one had heard from either boy all winter.

The next Sunday after Giuseppe Mango, Carmen Antonio, and Giovanni Pepe had arrived, the boys went to Zi Cesca and Zi Toro's home for an Italian dinner.

Zi Cesca, Giuseppe's first cousin, knew about the mohair shirt incident. He found they had much in common. For the first time, and with much ease, he spoke of his abuse at the hand of his father. Zi Cesca told Giuseppe many stories of his mother. During the next 55 years, until the end of their lives, Giuseppe and Zi Cesca remained very close friends.

In the spring of 1913, just like all of 1912, there were no positions open on the Erie, and none would be available until August of 1914. On the advice of a friend, Marco Illiuchi, Giuseppe, who considered himself a farmer, went to Cooperstown, New York. He boarded with Marco and his wife, and went to work for a German family as a gardener.

One rainy day, the German family asked him to come in and dry off. Because it was time for dinner they invited him to eat with them. Giuseppe graciously refused. He had noticed that the white food on their plates looked and smelled like potatoes.

When he returned to the boarding house he mentioned this to his Italian friend who agreed the family had been eating potatoes. Giuseppe snickered, "Americani mangiano patan" (Americans eat potatoes). After that, whenever Giuseppe talked about non-Italians, he referred to them as "mangia patan" (potato eaters).

Each month, when he got his pay, Giuseppe paid for his room and board, sent some money to his dad, and some to his brother in Susquehanna, to repay and thank him for buying his ticket to America. He saved all the rest.

After working six months he had budgeted his money so well he decided he could afford a motorcycle. He quickly learned how to drive it and rode it everywhere. It sure beat walking, until one snowy winter morning when he started down a steep hill. The road had a dusting of falling snow. Giuseppe was unaware that under this light blanket of snow there was a stretch of ice. When he hit the icy spot the motorcycle began to slide, he and the cycle parted company. As he slid on his back behind the cycle, he was afraid he would slam into it when it stopped. After about 100 feet the bike smashed through a snow bank Giuseppe braced himself to hit both the bank and the cycle. He came to a stop short of where the cycle had stopped.

Giuseppe got up, dusted himself off, and considered himself lucky that he had not gotten hurt. He left the motorcycle where it had stopped, and walked back home. He never again had any inclination to purchase or drive a motorcycle or automobile.

In early June of 1914, Lillo wrote they were hiring again on the Erie. Realizing how much he missed his brothers and friends, he thanked his German employer and the family he boarded with. The next morning he boarded a Delaware and Hudson train to Lanesboro.

The walk to Susquehanna from Lanesboro was refreshing. After greeting his brothers, he went to say hello to his first cousin Zi Cesca. She knew his birthday was on June 26, so she invited him to dinner the following Sunday, June 28.

At four that afternoon, Giuseppe arrived with his brothers. Everyone enjoyed Francesca's spaghetti and meatballs. Fresh fried hot peppers bought from Mike Pagano's grocery store went well with the meal. Over two gallons of wine was consumed. All those taking part in the feast could not remember when they had such an enjoyable time. Giuseppe and Pasquale had a memorable belated 19th birthday dinner.

Chapter
7 The Great War brings changes

World War One changed the landscape of Europe and changed the lives of many forever. Called "The Great War" because another war was unthinkable. The Central Powers: Germany, Austria-Hungary, Turkey and Bulgaria joined to fight against France, Britain, Russia, Italy, and 8 other Allied Countries. The German offensive started in 1914, and while the United States tried to stay out of it, the sinking of the Lusitania by German U-boats outraged American people. President Wilson wanted to stay out of Europe's war. Germany's overture to Mexico to become a fighting partner catapulted the United States into the war in 1917. In the four years of war, 10 million people were killed, 115,000 were Americans.

In 1918, after receiving his citizenship papers, and like many other Italian immigrants, Bernardino was drafted in the Army. The morning of November 11, 1918, he and his wife Millie, were tearfully saying goodbye at the railroad station. The telegraph operator came down the station platform with a paper in his hand. He called out for Bernardino and four other men who were there to board the train. He read what was on the paper. "The armistice was signed in France! The troop train was canceled and they could go home." The war to end all wars was over.

By the end of 1914, most Italians in Susquehanna were working full-time on the Erie Railroad. They were young, newly rich and much happiness prevailed. Life in America exceeded any dreams they had as young children in Italy. Because many sent money home, life in Italy for the older generation surpassed their earlier hopes as well. Meanwhile, the Italian community in Susquehanna continued to grow, not by new immigrants, but by the first American-born children.

Many of the homes in town had Victrola record players. All new Enrico Caruso records sold out quickly when they appeared on the Ryan and Alpaugh, Five and Ten Cent Store shelf.

Soon automobiles could be seen all over town. The new-fangled contraptions had to be pushed or pulled out of a mud hole or a snow bank with the help of several men. The sight of a model T Ford backing up a hill was not uncommon. The cars did not have a fuel pump at that time so they could not go forward up a hill. Gasoline would not feed to the engine because the gas line worked on gravity. Backing uphill solved the problem.

Il Progresso, an Italian newspaper printed in New York, was available and read by most Italians in Susquehanna. One of the featured articles included information about a new organization called the "Figli d'Italia," (Sons of Italy). Giuseppe Raddichi suggested to several Italians that a Susquehanna branch of that organization be formed. They applied for, and quickly received approval of their application from the Sons of Italy New York headquarters.

About 40 Italian men, originally from Giuliano and Moiano, including all the Mango boys, became charter members of the Susquehanna chapter of the Sons of Italy. Radicchi, so instrumental in forming the lodge, was elected their first president, a position he kept until his death in 1945.

The Sons of Italy band was a natural outgrowth of the lodge. It became one of the premier bands in Susquehanna's Fourth of July parade. A picture was taken of the band members in front of the Sons of Italy lodge just before the big parade on July 4th, sometime in the 1920s.

Life continued to change for the Mango brothers as well. Lillo, Pietro and Cicco, who had all saved enough money to be comfortable in Italy, decided to return to live there. Giuseppe still favored Italy, Bernardino and Pasquale decided to stay in the United States.

Raffaele Oropallo's trouble with the law, mentioned in a previous chapter, interested all the Italians in town. Zi Pasquale told the story to his oldest son Chuck. What Chuck remembers of the story is sketchy: An Irish girl, Patricia, lived with her family across the river in Oakland. One day, while shopping in downtown Susquehanna, she noticed Raffaele, who was tall, muscular and handsome, and quickly took a liking to him. Thereafter, whenever Raffaele was downtown, Patricia was also there. It was not long before they had gotten to know each other.

Patricia's father was a tough old Irishman who disliked the Italians, "Dagos or wops" as he called them. His greatest nightmare was that a daughter of his might marry one. He advised all three daughters that he did not want to see any of them anywhere near the "heathens" in Susquehanna. He was thankful his family lived in Oakland and the Italians, for the most part, stayed on their side of the river.

Patricia's great interest in Raffaele was no secret to the Italians, and to almost everyone else in town. Occasionally they were seen together and their relationship progressed. Early one warm summer evening, Raffaele met Patricia at a popular scenic spot on the riverbank in Oakland.

As they sat watching the river, Patricia and Raffaele soon, either voluntarily or not, got into a very compromising situation. As luck would have it, down the river three hundred feet from where the lovers were, Patricia's aunt and uncle, who never took an evening stroll, were walking along the river. Catching a glimpse of them from the corner of her eye, Patricia began yelling "rape." Raffaele, who did not understand what she was saying, decided he'd best discontinue his actions and quickly left the scene.

Patricia pressed charges and he was arrested for rape. Raffaele made bail and was released to the custody of his sister Francesca to await the trial. It was not hard for Raffaele's older brother, Francesco, to get moral and financial support of the other Italians in town. Many Italians donated money to hire an attorney, even though they believed he was dumb to have gotten involved with an Irish girl in the first place.

The trial was held in Montrose, the Susquehanna county seat. Most in town knew that Patricia had aggressively pursued Raffaele for some time. They also did not believe Patricia's story that on the evening in question she was walking alone on the riverbank when Raffaele attacked her.

After an emotional two-week trial the jury found Raffaele guilty. The judge put him on probation for one year. The Italians and many others felt that even probation was harsh punishment. At the end of his probation period Raffaele left Susquehanna. He eventually settled in Newark, New Jersey where he was married and thereafter led an exemplary life.

Chapter
8 *Giuseppe & Maddalena*

As a young man in Moiano, Giuseppe saw Maddalena at Mass each Sunday. Soon after he arrived in America he decided to write to her. To his surprise, he received a reply to his letter. Thereafter he wrote to her regularly. In one of his letters Giuseppe wrote that when he returned to Italy, he wanted to talk to her about something serious.

After the war ended, with marriage on his mind, Giuseppe returned to Italy. He left Susquehanna on Erie number 6 early in the morning of March 8, 1919. When he crossed the Hudson River on the Erie ferry to Chamber Street, there were many steamships either being towed to their pier or waiting for a tow. Just in front of the ferry a large liner went by. The decks were full of soldiers, who were loud and happy to see their homeland again. It surprised Giuseppe there still were American troops returning from France.

To save money he had booked passage on an old bucket, a freighter that carried passengers. It was much smaller than the one he had come to America on in 1913.

After stops at Halifax, Lisbon, Gibraltar, and Palermo, he arrived in Naples early on the morning of April 18. With a heavy suitcase in each hand, and much money in his pocket, he decided to walk to Moiano. It was a cool day so he stopped very little along the way. By four that afternoon he was on the road to his hometown.

Much in Moiano seemed different; he noticed things now that he had never noticed before. His heart jumped when Rosalie Saccone, who was filling her water bucket at the town well, smiled and shouted, "Buon venuto Peppino Mango." Giuseppe proudly returned the salute; he felt important that she recognized him so quickly. He headed directly to his old home. His father was sitting alone outside, eating a bowl of beans and struggling to chew a piece of hard bread.

Excited to see his dad after six years, he proudly gave him two shirts with two pairs of trousers, and a new wallet, which had an American twenty-dollar bill in it. It hurt and upset him that his dad just nodded his approval when he received the presents. He did not appear excited to see him.

Giuseppe visited with him for about 30 minutes and then went to the Palma home. Seeing the tall, dark eyed beauty with long hair ended any reluctance on his part. He decided that when the time was right he would ask her to marry him.

The rest of April and May he helped his dad *coppa monte*, and found his father had not changed. The burden of worrying about what he might do or say to trigger his dad's anger became more and more difficult.

By the middle of June, he asked to talk to Giovanni Palma, Maddalena's father. Giovanni consented to the marriage, however he extracted a promise from him that he would not take his daughter to America but to remain in Italy.

On July 14, Giuseppe and Maddalena were married in the municipio (the municipal building). The following day, Tuesday July 15, 1919, they were married in Santo Pietro Apostolo Catholic Church. As they walked down the church aisle he saw the empty pew where his mother and brothers used to sit when they went to Sunday mass. He could not help but think of his mother and how happy she would have been to see him grown-up and getting married.

Giuseppe and Maddalena (my father and mother) were complete opposites. He was about 5 feet 5 inches tall and as a young man he was thin and muscular. However, in every other way he was a big man. To earn a living, he worked any job no matter how hard it was. He was fiercely loyal to his father and brothers. So loyal, he had little awareness of any criticism or disloyalty they directed toward him. He talked very little about his feelings, his word was uncompromising, and he did not concern himself with other people's business.

Maddalena was 5 feet 7 inches tall; she liked to talk and she was very lazy. Maddalena received all the attention from her doting father. Spoiling her even more were her three older brothers, who treated their only sister like a princess. She always said people were good if they worked very hard. However, not much of this talk about a hard work ethic rubbed off on her, because she did not work very hard as a young girl at home. Nevertheless, because of the difficulties she found later in life, she had to work, like it or not, and she worked hard all her married life.

After the wedding Giuseppe stayed in the Palma household. Having meals prepared on a regular basis was a luxury he enjoyed. He asked Maddalena to prepare a meal each Sunday for his father and it pleased him to take it to him. This did not improve his dad's attitude towards him. Giuseppe finally gave up his desire to get along with his father. His father rejected him as a child and rejected him as an adult as well.

Giuseppe convinced Maddalena's father that they must go to America where he could earn more money. Then he could save enough and return to Italy to raise a family. Maddalena's father was not hard to convince, because he once did the same thing.

Giuseppe also convinced Maddalena's brother, Filippo, that America was a good place to work and earn money. Filippo took Giuseppe's advice and finally immigrated to America in 1921.

Early Monday morning January 12, 1920, Giuseppe hired a white and blue surrey pulled by a horse. Maddalena, who had never traveled more than 10 miles from Moiano, enjoyed the 21-mile trip to Naples.

As the surrey neared the sea front in Naples, Maddalena saw a very large ship, already docked, with a white star on both smoke stacks. On the ship's bow was its name *"Dante Alighieri."* She knew that the ship was named after a famous Italian poet and writer.

The *Dante Alighieri* sailed from Genoa late Saturday evening, January 10, 1920. It left Naples on Monday afternoon, January 12, and arrived in New York 17 days later on Thursday morning, January 29, 1920.

All Italian line ships traversing from Genoa, Naples, and Palermo, to New York, always left Italy with a full load of passengers. The *Dante Alighieri,* which did not stop in Palermo, carried 43 first-cabin and 239 second-cabin, for a total of 282 passengers. They were in "secondo economia" (second economic class). Even though Maddalena lived well at home, the cabin was quite large and she felt like a "regina"(queen) arriving in Naples in style, and leaving on such a modern and fast ship.

The ship's crew paid much attention to her, because she did not get seasick. They called her "marinara" (sailor). She roamed the entire ship over that 17-day period. She remembered eating beefsteaks and being asked if she wanted a drink that she had never had before. The cost at the time was 5¢ a glass. She immediately decided she liked this drink called beer. Drinking beer and eating beefsteaks was her favorite food and drink on her first trip to America. Early on the morning of Thursday, January 29, on the deck with his new bride, with the New York skyline in front of them, Giuseppe looked over at Maddalena and proclaimed, "Guaglie, guarda la Statua di Libertà," (girl, look there, the Statue of Liberty).

The *Dante Alighieri* docked on pier 18 in New York harbor. As usual, all second cabin passengers boarded a ferry that took them directly to Ellis Island. That first trip to America for Maddalena was the best time she would have for the rest of her life. A very hard life, not at all like she may have imagined, was awaiting her.

The ship's registry listed Giuseppe as a non-immigrant. At Ellis Island, Giuseppe waited patiently outside for four hours, for his wife to clear the trauma of the Ellis Island immigration station. That afternoon they happily boarded the ferry for The Battery.

From The Battery they rushed to the elevated train station to catch the next uptown train. Maddalena was able to catch a view of the New York skyline before the train went underground. After several stops, Giuseppe picked up their luggage and motioned for her to follow him and they got off at the Chamber Street Station. Once up out of the subway, Maddalena could again see the skyline. The scene was different, but it was still New York.

Since it was after 3:00 p.m., and too late to catch Erie No. 3 from Jersey City, Giuseppe hired a horse and carriage and he took his bride to Mulberry Street. He wanted to buy her Italian treats, but before he could do so, his new bride started to barter with Italian shop owners. She would not let him buy apples from an Italian with a Sicilian accent, who displayed apples on his pushcart. She had seen the same kind of apples in a store window that were cheaper.

Dad asked the carriage driver, who had waited for them, to take them for a drive around the New York City streets. Maddalena enjoyed this very much. There were more automobiles, streetcars and trucks than she had ever seen. Large buildings were everywhere, and there were so many people. By 6:00 p.m., it was dark and cold when the driver let them off at the foot of Chamber Street, where they boarded the ferry for Jersey City.

The warm Jersey City station was a welcome relief. Soon the station announcer proclaimed, "Westbound passenger train for Patterson, Passaic, Middletown, Port Jervis, Callicoon, Hancock, Deposit, Susquehanna, Binghamton, Elmira, Hornell, and Buffalo, now loading on track 6." All strange words to Maddalena, but she did recognize the word Susquehanna among the jumble of English.

Even though Giuseppe had been away from work for 10 months, the conductor on No. 5 honored his Erie Pass. After crossing the ocean on a ship, Maddalena was taking her first train ride. They arrived in Susquehanna at 1:15 a.m., and it was very cold. Maddalena was happy her mother had insisted she pack the heavy sweater she placed over her other clothes.

They walked up the inside steps of the station out on Front Street, then up the steps to Main Street. As they walked up Main Street, Giuseppe neglected to tell Maddalena the glassy, dark spots on the sidewalk were patches of ice and were slippery. Maddalena slipped and fell; she landed with a thud on her backside. The fall did not hurt her much, but she was terribly embarrassed. Good thing it was late at night, no one saw her fall. She looked daggers at Giuseppe for not warning her of the ice.

The next morning Maddalena went outside for a fresh look at Susquehanna and her new neighborhood. The milk delivery man, seeing this attractive Italian woman for the first time, decided to be friendly and shouted "Good morning," to her. Good morning sounds similar to an Italian swear word, Maddalena could not understand why he would be swearing at her.

Maddalena never did like Susquehanna; it was cold, snowed in the winter, and rained all year-round. There was constant humidity in the summer and winter. Cellars, in most of the homes where they lived, filled with water after a heavy rain. The houses were so damp, mildew formed on walls and furniture in the upstairs bedrooms. Most of the homes did not have indoor plumbing.

For the next two years Giuseppe worked steadily on the railroad. Maddalena made many friends with her neighbors, both Italian and American. Giuseppe never tired of Maddalena's cooking. Pasta, meatballs, polenta, and pasta e fasul, were all favorites of his. All of the foods he liked were affordable and prepared regularly in America.

On September 19, 1920, their first child, Liberata Marie, was born two months premature. Her health was a problem for the first two months of her life, and then she grew strong and healthy. Marie was a good child and at an early age, she helped her mother with chores around the house. By the time she was 5 years old, she began to sew simple dresses for herself. When the rest of the Mango children were growing up, Marie was like a second mother to them.

Of the three Mango sons who remained in America, Pasquale was the last to marry. With marriage on his mind, he headed back to Italy in August of 1920. He stayed with his father, but helped as little as possible and did his best to ignore him. Early in 1921, Rose Cuozo, a bright and sensible young maiden, consented to marry him.

Giovanni Mango, sensing he would lose another son to America, treated Pasquale very well. As the old man chewed and puffed on his cigar he told Pasquale they should work the land *coppa monte* and share the harvest. Pasquale may have considered it, but when his wife announced she was pregnant, he quickly decided to leave for America. He bid his father and Rose's parents farewell. Pasquale, Rose, and their unborn son Charles Angelo left for America.

In 1922, with a strike looming on the railroads, Maddalena was homesick for Italy and her family. She asked Giuseppe if they could go for a visit. The Giuseppe Mango family, husband, wife, and one daughter headed for New York. He remembered his promise to his father in-law, and was determined to keep an open mind about living in Italy again.

At the same time, Giuseppe's brothers Lillo, Pietro, and Cicco, were returning to Italy on the same ship. They never returned to America. Pasquale and Bernardino accompanied their brothers to New York. All six brothers had a meal together in a small Italian restaurant on Mulberry Street. During this meal there was much sadness because each one knew this probably would be the last time all six would be together.

In Italy, while Maddalena visited her parents, Giuseppe visited his father. He was surprised to be ordered to look after Lillo's children. Giuseppe snapped back at his father and told him he came to visit not baby-sit. Now that his father had three sons home with him, he cared even less for Giuseppe. He told Lillo and Cicco they could share harvest from their land *coppa monte*. This extinguished any thought Giuseppe had for staying in Italy. Pietro worked with his father in-law, and had enough land to support himself and his wife. Had Giuseppe decided to stay in Italy, he would have no land to till. Although he had money to buy land, none was for sale.

The day before they were to depart Moiano, Giuseppe told his father he would stop to say good-bye early the next morning, before he left to go *coppa monte*. Giuseppe, always true to his word, went to bid him farewell early in the morning. His dad was not home. He looked up the path and could see his father far ahead, walking very fast for coppa monte. He hollered, "Tadi" (daddy) but his father did not turn. Giuseppe stood there for a long time hoping that his father would turn around, but he soon disappeared around a small bend in the path.

Giuseppe began to follow slowly; he reached the fig tree where, as a child, he had eaten those green figs. Looking at it more closely, he could see the tree had aged and had many dead branches. It did not have as much fruit as it used to have. He remembered that after the figs ripened the tree was a source of good eating. He and his brothers used to gorge themselves with them, these being the few times they completely satisfied their hunger as children.

He stood silently for quite a while debating if he should run and catch up with his father to say goodbye. At the speed his dad was walking he would have had to run all the way *coppa monte* to catch up with him. He turned around and walked back to his father's dwelling. He went over to the pot of beans on the fire. He realized that the pot his dad used to cook beans was the same pot in which Peppino had let the beans burn 17 years ago. His dad had gotten smarter; the pot was full with water to the very top. He could see that by 12:00 or 1:00 in the afternoon when the fire went out, the beans would have not burned and would be edible. He wondered why his dad hadn't thought of it years ago. Pausing momentarily, he was tempted to empty the water and lets the beans burn. At the same time he felt much pity for his dad, he had gotten old, had no one to cook for him, and his diet was still mostly beans and hard bread. He lived alone with no one to take care of him when he was sick. Giuseppe vowed that he would send even more money to him in the future.

He was thankful that in America he had all the food he wanted. There was plenty of work, to earn money to raise his family and he had a good wife and child. He slowly started to walk away from his childhood home. He stopped several times, turned and looked at that stone hut; how small, empty and cold it looked. There was pain in his heart as his childhood memories came more into focus. His dad had thoroughly rejected him back then and he had rejected him for the last time that morning. Before rounding the bend in the street he turned once more to look at the hut and the cooking beans. He sensed the great emptiness of his childhood after his mother died. That small stone hut, and Moiano, was not his home anymore. And had not been for many years.

He felt foolish to have returned to Italy at all. At his father-in-law's home, he picked up Maddalena and Marie and headed for Naples. Maddalena, who had only good memories, promised her mother and father she would visit again and tearfully departed.

Giuseppe had his Erie Railroad pass so Ellis Island posed no problems for the Mango family. A friend of Maddalena's also came to America with her daughter. She was denied entry at Ellis Island because she had become ill on the ship. She asked Maddalena to take her child and notify the child's father in Mendham, New Jersey, to come and get her.

When they arrived in Susquehanna, they found the railroad strike had become very bitter. Pickets were around the station and all the other railroad property. Giuseppe telegraphed the little girl's father, to tell him that he had his daughter, and gave him his address. The girl's father came on the Erie train to Susquehanna. When he got off the train, being Italian and not familiar to the pickets, they assumed that he came to work. They were furious, and one pulled a gun on the poor man. Giuseppe arrived just in time to explain that the man was there to pick up his daughter and not to work.

There was much violence in most railroad shop towns, including Susquehanna, during the 1922 strike. President Harding and congress advised the railroads in February that they must cut freight rates by 10 per cent. At the same time the shop crafts unions were asking for a 12% pay increase for one million of their shop workers throughout the United States.

By March 2, the railroad unions were threatening strike. At the same time the coal miners, who had no love for the railroads, started wildcat strikes in Illinois and Ohio. Conversely, many of the railroads depended heavily on revenue received for hauling coal. The strikes by the miners reduced the amount of coal tonnage hauled, reducing the railroads income. This in turn caused the railroads to lay off workers.

On May 24, the government ordered the railroads to cut freight rates by 10%. The railroads then asked that their employee's take a 10% cut in pay. At the same time, the railroads proposed the elimination of seniority rights, which the unions vigorously opposed.

Aggravating an already bad situation, many coal mines closed in early June. Two weeks later the railroad shop workers went on strike.

Eager to go back to work, settlement of the wage issue in August gave the workers renewed hope. The railroad executives still insisted that seniority rights must be eliminated. On September 14, 1922, the strike ended, without changes to the long-fought for seniority rules. The next day, September 15, Giuseppe went back to work in the roundhouse. He kept his seniority and now could hold the position of boilermaker helper.

Another daughter, Giovannina, was born on April 6, 1923. She became her parent's favorite child. Giovannina was a very bright child. Like Marie, she was calm and was no problem for mother. By the time she was 18 months old she tried to help her mother and Marie wash dishes. Her mother would tap her on the backside and tell her to get away, saying she was too small to help. On October 22, 1924, a third daughter, Nanine (Anna) was born.

During the 1920s, prosperity attended most families. Giuseppe and many other Italians were active members of the Sons of Italy. At the meetings the Italians discussed common problems. They played bocce in the summer and played cards the rest of the year. Scopa and briscola were their favorite card games.

For other entertainment, and at any get together, Italian men could be seen playing a game they called morra. Morra needed no more than one hand. Two or more could play it, but for the most part, only two played. The object of the game was to guess a number one to ten. Each player in the game hollered a number, as each simultaneously extended their hand and displayed, zero, one, two, three, four or five fingers. If you showed three fingers and hollered five and your opponent showed two fingers, and hollered any other number, you got a point, the first player to get seven points won.

Another simpler form of morra was "para e spara" (odd and even). The player who got the point when he correctly guessed the total number of fingers displayed, were odd or even. These games were simple yet challenging. I remember my dad and other Italians playing morra at least through the 1940s.

Although prohibition became law on January 16, 1920, the Italians, and many others, made their own home brew. To the Italians, wine was considered more a food, because it was served at every meal, than a social or intoxicating drink. In Binghamton, they bought boxes of grapes every fall, which were shipped from California. Then they made their own wine. Thus, until 1933 when prohibition ended, Italians always had homemade wine to drink.

Even though selling alcohol was illegal, beer and hard liquor were still plentiful. Susquehanna had at least three speakeasies, which their two policemen not only ignored, but patronized as well.

Susquehanna improved its streets considerably during the 1920s. Because cars replaced horses, old dirt roads were replaced with new brick surfaces, including all of Main Street and other streets. Automobile tires on a speeding car made a whining sound as they went up and down West Main Street on that brick pavement.

In the mid-west, during the 1920s, there was a resurgence of the Ku Klux Klan (KKK). This KKK action seemed to target Jewish immigrants who had arrived from Russia in the 1880s. Much of the Northeast, after the renewal of the KKK, stayed free of this radical group.

Susquehanna, however, joined the south and the mid-west and developed their own local branch of the KKK. Without Negroes to harass, they still had Italians and Catholics.

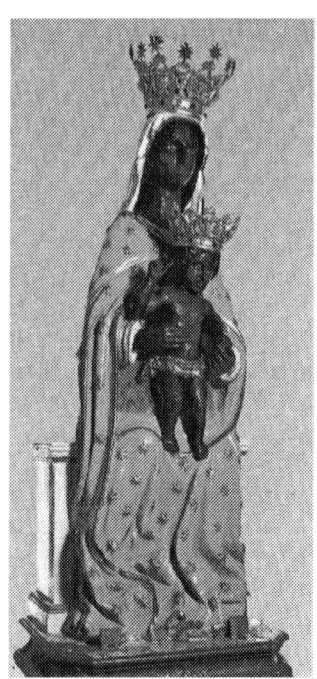

Madonna Della Libera
(Our Lady of Freedom Moiano)

Grandfather Giovanni Mango 1932

Grandmother Palma 1951

Courtesy Peabody Essex Museum
Italian Line Dante Aligheri, S. S. built 1915

Courtesy Peabody Essex Museum
Italian Line Principe Di Piemonte, S. S. Built 1907

Susquehanna station view from west of the station 1913

Susquehanna station view from east of the station 1913

Giuseppe Mango Family 1923 Standing Marie
On Mother's lap is the first Giovannina

Giuseppe Mango family 1925 standing left, the first Giovannina, seated on mother's lap Anna, and standing right Marie

The Sons of Italy band members. The photograph was taken in the middle 1920s in front of the Old Canawacta and The Standing Eagle Hotel – Front row, L to R   Felice Pagano, William Canini, Joe Caruso, Salvatore Mauro, Joseph Orlando, Dominic Caso, Angelo Battisti, unknown*, Michael Pagano, Angelo Calogloia, and Fernando Pacifica. Middle row L to R Paul Morelli, Prosper Pagano, Americus Gabriele, Louis Galotto, Pasquale Valentine, Nicholas Napolitano, Giuseppe Parrillo, Giuseppe Mango, and Christopher Delucia Top row L to R Liberto Parrillo, Giovanni Parrillo Parrillo, Vito Cianfriglia, Frank Napolitano, Pasquale Mango, young Philip Radicchi, and Giuseppe Radicchi. *A paisano visiting from Binghamton got into the picture, his name his unknown.

Chapter

9 *Maddalena and daughters visit Italy*

In 1925 Maddalena was very homesick. She asked Giuseppe if they could visit Italy. He answered that she could go with the girls. He was happy and experiencing the best period in his life; he did not want to return to the sadness of his childhood.

Maddalena at age 28 was prosperous, intelligent, and confident. She boarded a ship with her three daughters headed for Italy, in early July of 1925. Aboard the ship she became upset when the infant son of a woman she had met on the boat died of the measles. Little did she know she would soon lose a child of her own, from the same disease.

Marie was almost 5, Giovannina 2, and Anna at eight months, developed fevers and respiratory problems. In Naples, Maddalena hired a cab to take her and the girls to the railroad station where they boarded a train to Arpaia. At Arpaia, her brother Nicole was waiting for them.

After they arrived in Moiano, all three girls had the black measles. Marie and Anna got better, but Giovannina did not. Anna was soon crawling all over the house; no one could stop her. Marie, a mature 5 year-old, began to help her grandmother with the house chores.

The doctor frowned when he saw how sick two year-old Giovannina was. He told Maddalena her child might not get better. His prescription was to keep the child indoors and warm.

For two weeks, Maddalena did all she could for her. She continually prayed to the Madonna Della Libera to help her little girl get well. Each day she got progressively worse. One evening when Maddalena picked up Giovannina to comfort her, she screamed, "Dio Mio, Dio Mio" (My God, My God). Grandfather ran to get the doctor and was back with him in less than 10 minutes. On August 8, 1925, Giovannina, the big sister I never knew died.

Maddalena's parents were very distressed. All they could do was to try and comfort their daughter. Her father wrote to Giuseppe telling him, as best he could, of Giovannina's death.

There was a Mass for the baby in the Parrocchia Di Santo Pietro Apostolo (the parish of St. Peter the Apostle). It was the same church Maddalena and Giuseppe had attended as children, and had taken their marriage vows, seven years ago. Maddalena, unable to cope with the loss of a child, asked Nicole to book return passage to America.

Maddalena's father, worried that his letter would not arrive in America in time, sent a cable to Giuseppe advising of the circumstances of Giovannina's death, the ship and time of arrival in New York. He instructed Giuseppe to wait at the Jersey City Erie Passenger terminal for Maddalena. One week later, her parents and brother, Nicole, accompanied Maddalena and the girls to the Naples dock.

As the ship pulled away from Naples harbor, while holding her two girls, Maddalena cried as she watched her parents and brother Nicole become smaller in the distance as they waved goodbye. She had deep regrets of having come to Italy at all, and silently vowed never to return.

For the next 17 days she left the cabin only to take the girls for meals, while she ate very little. There was no joy for Maddalena during this crossing of the Atlantic. She could not face the fact that she was leaving part of herself behind. She would not have a grave to visit where she could honor her little girl. A child to whom she had given life was not part of their little family anymore.

The ship docked in New York at ten in the morning, in early September 1925. She and the girls were the first passengers off the ship. She quickly hired a cab, being closer to 23rd Street; she went there for the 23rd Street ferry to Jersey City.

While the ferry was docking at the Erie Terminal, she could see the forlorn figure of her husband in the distance. A feeling of warmth went through her when she noticed that he had spotted her and the girls, as he began walking toward them.

At the Jersey City station they bought cake and a glass of milk for the girls. As Marie devoured her cake, Maddalena fed Anna little pieces of cake by hand. Anna had no problem eating the cake and drinking milk from a glass. Giuseppe and Maddalena managed to smile, and were deeply thankful for their two remaining healthy little girls.

They left Jersey City on Erie No. 3, at 3:00 p.m. On the train they turned one of the seats around so they would have two double seats facing each other. The Mango family was home at 9:00 that evening and both girls were asleep in a warm bed by 9:30.

Maddalena never forgot the loss of Giovannina. In later years she recounted that Giovannina, as small as she was, would ask to help with the dishes and how she tapped the child on the backside and would tell her to get out of the way. Maddalena always believed her baby might not have died if they had not gone to Italy.

Maddalena's brother Filippo, who boarded with them since his arrival in 1921, tried to help his sister. He spoke to Maddalena and Giuseppe and said that there were children who died of the dreaded black measles in Susquehanna. They could have been infected before they left for Italy.

Soon Maddalena was with child again. Filippo came home each day with a large beefsteak for her to prepare so they could all share it. That was good for everyone especially Maddalena and her unborn child. On Easter Sunday afternoon, April 17, 1927, at 5:00 in the evening, she gave birth to a healthy and fat son, and I was named Giovanni.

That evening Dr. Seth Miller came to see Maddalena and smiled when he saw the newly born healthy little boy. Americanizing the name, the doctor wrote "John" on my birth certificate instead of Giovanni. The following week, I was baptized at St. John's Catholic Church.

The Southern Italian tradition was to name the first male child after the grandfather. In this case, I was the second Mango child to be named after both grandfathers. (Giovannina is the feminine of John). I am also the second John Mango mentioned in these pages. The other, of course, is grandfather Giovanni Mango, whom I never met.

Although I was born very healthy and fat, I did not remain that way. As a child I was just skin and bones. Anemia and ear problems were with me all my young life. My ear problems finally ended when I was 12 years old however, the anemia continues to be a problem.

Shortly after I was born, a fourth son, Anthony, was born to Zi Pasquale and Zi Rose. In the spring of 1928, baby Anthony became seriously ill.

My father suggested we visit little Anthony, but my mother was opposed to it. She pleaded with Aunt Millie, Uncle Bernardino's wife, to help change his mind. Aunt Millie told him, "Joseph, your children can catch that sickness if they go near little Anthony. Listen to your wife, go yourself, but leave your children at home."

Nevertheless, that evening our whole family went to Zi Pasquale's home and visited a very sick Anthony. The following morning little Anthony was dead. Three days later I began to cough. The next morning I was so sick, dad asked Dr. Miller to come to our house to examine me.

The doctor gave mother cough medicine for me and told her to keep me warm. Very soon I was as sick as little Anthony had been. Mother couldn't help but remember little Giovannina and how ill she was before she died. Mother prayed to God not to let her lose another one of her children. My dad ran downtown to get the doctor. When he arrived he examined me, a little one-year old child gasping for each breath. He told my mother her only hope was to keep putting damp hot pads on my chest.

Mother followed the doctor's instructions. She kept the pads on my chest all that day, all night, and only left my side to get another hot pad. The pads hung above a boiling pan of water on the kitchen cook stove.

The next morning I was a little better. Dad, who had stayed home to take care of Anna and Marie, went downtown and again returned with Dr. Miller. The doctor looked at me and smiled, I certainly had improved.

On March 1, 1929, another girl was born. It seemed to mother and father that Giovannina was returned to them. And so they named their fifth child Giovannina.

Chapter
10 *Working on the Erie Railroad*

The accidental death of many Italian workers, in or near the roundhouse, during the early part of the 20th century, troubled and haunted the hearts of all the Italians in Susquehanna.

Steam engines came to the ash pit under their own power. Ashes were still red hot when they were removed. Any worker near the ash pit tried to be up wind so he would not breathe in the soft coal gas.

The death of Angelo Tolomei, in 1926, was especially disturbing. Angelo worked the 3:00 to 11:00 p.m. shift. One evening at 10:30, Angelo and a co-worker finished removing ashes from the last engine (In fact, it would be late the following morning, before another engine arrived at the ash pit). When Angelo did not return home by seven the next morning, his wife went to the roundhouse to look for him. The foreman told her that Angelo went home after his shift last night. A search was conducted in and around the roundhouse. It wasn't long before he was found in the ash pit. How, or what caused him to fall into it was never established. It remains a mystery to this day.

Carmen Antonio Oropallo came to the United States in March of 1913, with my father and Giovanni Pepe. On Thursday, March 22, 1928, at the ash pit, he was between and below the cab and tender of engine 3116. Using a hammer to hit a defective valve that operated the grates under the engine firebox, he apparently missed and hit a steam pipe, causing an explosion of steam. Workers in the roundhouse heard Carmen's scream and ran outside. As the steam dissipated, they could clearly see Carmen Antonio lying between the rails under the engine tender, next to the pit. Steam came out of his clothes as though his body was on fire. My father was the first to crawl near Carmen; he tried to remove Carmen's jacket but it was too hot. At the same time, he saw that flesh from his arm and neck had loosened from the bone. An Irishman, named Jack, said he would use his truck to take Carmen Antonio to the hospital. My father hollered for someone to get a large board that was nearby. Zi Giovanni (Carmen's brother), who had just arrived, dragged the board behind him as he crawled to where Carmen and my dad were. Dad and Zi Giovanni tugged at Carmen's less injured arm, and after much effort, they were barely able to get him securely on the board. They then dragged the board with Carmen on it over the rail and away from the engine. At that point, Jack arrived in his Model T Ford truck.

Four men squeezed themselves and the plank on the truck bed. Jack then instructed them to hold the plank with their hands over their legs while sitting on the bed of the truck, thus cushioning the ride for Carmen. Jack went as fast as he could, driving carefully over two rails, then down the dirt road to the street. Blowing his horn to warn other vehicles to stay out of his way, he went through the only traffic light in town as he made a left on Main Street, and headed up east Main St. to Barnes Hospital. At the hospital front door the medical staff took over.

Doctor Miller told the Italians to go back to work. Carmen, who was still coherent, thanked all his fellow workers. In the hospital, as Doctor Miller and the nurse cut off his clothes, it was evident that much of his upper body flesh on his left side was virtually cooked by the steam. At the roundhouse not much work was done; all afternoon the men discussed the accident.

By the next day, Carmen's head had swollen so much he could not open his mouth or eyes. Still coherent, he asked that they bring his son to see him. Zi Filippo, who was there at the time, went down church hill, ran up Main Street to Carmen's home, where a neighbor was taking care of four-month old Alfonso. Zi Filippo covered the infant as he quickly walked three miles back to the hospital. Carmen's wife and his brother, Giovanni, who were at his side night and day, held little Alfonso on Carmen's stomach. Carmen attempted to move his arm to touch him but could not. However, he could feel his son's weight and managed a weak smile. Shortly after that, Carmen lapsed into a coma. By the grace of God, the loss of consciousness released him from the excruciating pain. Early Sunday morning March 25, 1928, Carmen stopped breathing. Grief-stricken by the loss of Carmen, the other Italians could barely concentrate at work. My mother comforted my father and Zi Filippo as best she could.

Early in this story we told of Zi Fiore Oropallo, who went to Susquehanna in 1902. Because at that time there was no work available in Susquehanna, he rode freight trains to Florence, Kentucky, and lived there for the next 26 years. After being diagnosed with a terminal illness in early 1928, he decided to leave his common law wife, and return to Italy to ask for his wife's forgiveness. He arrived unannounced in Susquehanna. The train trip had taken its toll. He knew he would never make it to Italy. Learning of the recent tragic death of his younger son, and distraught that he never received forgiveness from him, he went to see his other son, Zi Giovanni.

Zi Giovanni's wife said she did not want a sick person in her house. Furthermore, she said she did not want him there because, years before, he had abandoned his wife and young children in Italy. Zi Giovanni, who was at work, could have overruled his wife's decision when he returned home, but did not. Zi Fiore died 2 months later.

Zi Fiore told Zi Cesca that after his death, she would know of Zi Giovanni's punishment, for not helping or allowing him to ask for forgiveness.

A month after his father's death, Zi Giovanni was in the cab of a steam engine at the firebox, breaking up the clinkers with an iron rod. The wooden stop of an over-loaded coal tender broke and coal rapidly filled the engine cab, and temporarily trapped him near the open door of the firebox. For more than two minutes he inhaled firebox gases, as he frantically dug his way to the engine cab window. His lungs were seriously injured. He suffered from emphysema for the rest of his life. Zi Giovanni, for whom I had great respect, died in March of 1966, of complications due to emphysema.

Two years after Zi Giovanni's accident, on the morning of March 19, 1930, it snowed heavily for several hours. Anyone who has ever worked on a railroad, knows that when there is snow on the ground, especially newly fallen snow, it becomes a great muffler of sound. About all one can hear when a freight train passes is the clicking of the wheels on the rail joints.

Salvatore Ficarro was a track foreman. He and his men were replacing the south rail of the westbound track on the street overpass downtown, about half a mile east of the station. Not only were the regular railroad noises greatly muffled due to the storm, visibility was also very poor. Salvatore was in a hurry to get the job done. No. 1, the westbound Erie Limited, was on time and due in 20 minutes.

The switch engine assigned to the westbound yards was on its way and hurried for the JA tower. The JA tower was in Lanesboro, located about two miles east of the station. Salvatore, who had been helping his men, was standing between the east and westbound tracks. He never heard the switch engine when he got up and leaned toward the eastbound track. The switch engine, going about 25 miles per hour, hit him. He died in Barnes Hospital four days later. Young Pat Parrillo, who visited him in the hospital, said that Salvatore told him the pain was so bad he wished that someone would get a gun and shoot him.

Frances Yanicelli, Salvatore's daughter, provided much of the details of her dad's accident. She said her dad did not come from Moiano or Giuliano. He was a Sicilian who settled in New York City. Later, when he wanted a quiet town to raise his family, they moved to Susquehanna. Salvatore was survived by his wife and nine children.

Salvatore Catalino was in the westbound yard, one cold, winter morning. He was on the last rail next to the river, near the roundhouse, working alone to remove a broken rail. The track had not been used all winter and was imbedded in ice. Salvatore was using a pick to break up the ice around the rail. The engineer of a nearby switch engine said that Salvatore had his back to the riverbank. As he lifted the pick over his head, he slipped or fell backwards down the bank and onto the frozen river. The ice broke and he fell through, into the freezing water. The engineer repeatedly blew the horn to get the attention of others in the roundhouse. Many from the roundhouse went down to the river, but there was no sign of Salvatore. Divers were called in; after hours of breaking ice and dragging the river they finally found his body. Frances Yanicelli, who was his child at home, remembers hearing the engine whistle blowing for four or five minutes. She said she still cannot stand the sound of railroad engine whistles.

Chapter
11 *Troubles on the Erie Railroad*

For the Erie Railroad in the 1920s, freight tonnage increased steadily, and the line was doing well. They replaced many of the old and dilapidated steam engines with newer and more efficient ones. The new steam engines carried the Erie into the era of diesel that, by the 1950s, was in full force.

Some of the success that the Erie Railroad experienced in the 1920s was directly attributable to two brothers in Cleveland, the Van Sweringens, who attempted to build a great railroad empire. Edward Hungerford, in his book "Men Of Erie," states that toward this end they seemed to have final success within their grasp. They had control of the Pere Marquette (PM), which had extensive trackage primarily in the state of Michigan.

They acquired full control of the New York, Chicago, and St. Louis Railroad (Nickel Plate Road NKP). The NKP ran from Buffalo along the south shore of Lake Erie, through Erie, Cleveland, Fort Wayne, and into Chicago, with branches to St. Louis and Peoria.

The Chesapeake and Ohio (C&O) went from Newport News, Richmond, and Ashland, to Chicago, with other branches in Virginia, Kentucky, Ohio and Indiana. The C&O was the richest of the rail lines. Most of their riches came from hauling coal. The C&O bought the stock of the other railroads to create the Van Sweringen Empire.

The Van Sweringens were also looking west to control the Missouri Pacific (MP). The MP was a consolidation of many smaller railroads. MP's mainline and many branches served such cities as St. Louis, Kansas City, Omaha, New Orleans, Houston and San Antonio.

The Erie was to be the Van Sweringen brothers' railroad empire gateway into the city of New York. It fit in well for the Erie connected with the NKP at Cleveland, Dunkirk and Buffalo. The planned acquisition of Erie included moving the headquarters from New York City to Cleveland.

In the late 1920s, even before the deaths of both Van Sweringens within weeks of each other, the railroad empire that would have covered 15,000 miles of railroad track went up in smoke. The C&O, NKP, PM, and the Erie were on their own again.

The Erie bought two new passenger trains, which went into service on June 2, 1929. The new 2900 steam passenger engines powered the trains. The new westbound train, the Erie Limited 1001, left Jersey City at 9:10 on Sunday morning, June 2, 1929, and each morning thereafter. The train made a two-minute stop in Susquehanna at 2:01 p.m., where the Susquehanna division train crew boarded at the station. At the coal pocket, while the engine tender was filled with coal and the water tank refilled, the Susquehanna division engine crew replaced the

Delaware division engine crew. Ten minutes later it was on its way to Chicago to arrive the next morning at 8:25.

That afternoon, when the new westbound Limited arrived, most of the shop workers went outside to see the train as it slowed to a stop at the station. Over a hundred people came to see the new train. Almost as many people were there the next afternoon when the new eastbound Limited arrived. The eastbound Limited, scheduled to leave Chicago at 5:35 in the late afternoon, stopped in Susquehanna the next afternoon at 2:16, and was scheduled to arrive in Jersey City early that evening at 7:10. Both trains east and westbound were due in Susquehanna within 15 minutes of each other.

For the trip up to Gulf Summit the eastbound Limited needed a helper engine, which was added to the front end of the train at the coal pocket. With the helper engine, the train made up enough time to the Summit so it could stop, uncouple the helper engine, and be on its way. Like everything the Erie did, and to use an expression of the time, "the line was always a day late and a dollar short." As stated earlier, the new Limited went into service on June 2, 1929, just four months before the market crash. After that, the Erie did not buy new passenger equipment. Between 1946 and 1953, much of the old equipment was remodeled in the Susquehanna shops.

In June of 1929, the shop superintendent tacked a notice on the bulletin board at the roundhouse, that advised closure of the Susquehanna shops, and that in the future, Hornell shops would do the work usually done in Susquehanna. Two weeks after the notice, a handful of men were laid off. The only effect it had on dad was that he had to work the 3:00 to 11:00 p.m. shift as a boilermaker helper. Zi Filippo took a job in the ash pit again, and he was also on the 3:00 to 11:00 p.m. shift.

My father refused to believe that moving the shops would affect his own employment. Because of the uphill grade to Gulf Summit, pusher engines would remain in Susquehanna. Light repairs on them would continue in Susquehanna. The Erie had just finished building a new turntable at the roundhouse to accommodate the big 3300 freight engines it was putting into service. This convinced my father that he would continue to have a job.

Zi Bernardino, not prone to fool himself, decided that there might be future employment problems if he stayed in Susquehanna. He advised his wife Millie of his decision, and they packed up and moved to Albany. He surmised it was a big city and there would be more work opportunities there for him to support his young family.

Most Italians in Susquehanna paid little attention that October, when the main topic of conversation was about the stock market crash. Most knew very little about stocks; to them it was just where the rich invested their money. They thought it was a problem for the wealthy, not for them. They surmised that it could have very little effect on Susquehanna or their families.

Chapter 12 *The Great Depression*

As a young child I had problems with sore throats, ear infections, and anemia. The anemia was complicated because I never felt hungry. Therefore, I ate very little. One evening, in the fall of 1930, I became dizzy and fell down, due to my anemic condition. Then I began to hallucinate. I saw the bucket of coal next to the kitchen stove, and I thought it was a dog, and I feared the dog was going to bite me.

Doctor Seth Miller diagnosed my problem as anemia. He instructed mother to give my sisters and me a spoon of Scott's Emulsion, or cod liver oil, every day. Both oils tasted terrible and it was an effort for us to swallow it. But after taking it on a regular basis, I no longer had hallucinations, and had few problems with anemia for the remainder of my childhood.

Although the anemia was alleviated, the sore throats and ear infections were not. Another physician, Dr. Condon, said my sore throats and ear infections would clear up with the removal of my tonsils and adenoids. He told my father to take me to a specialist in Binghamton.

The morning before Christmas, father and I walked down to the railroad station where we waited on the station platform for the train. Soon I could see the westbound passenger train coming toward us; a big steam engine belching steam and smoke. The drive wheels of the engine were twice as high as I was tall, and very frightening to a youngster like myself.

While I looked outside the train window, as it headed for Binghamton, I noticed the cars on the highway; some seemed to be racing with the train. Most of all, I perceived them as being like toys and I told dad how small they were.

I do not remember the specialist or being in his office, but I do remember walking back to the train station later that afternoon. We stopped in a large market on Chenango Street (the Mohegan Market), where dad bought fish.

It had gotten very cold; rain, sleet, and some snow were falling. From the market it was a long, cold, four-city block walk to the station. Years later I would come to know how bad the weather could be in Binghamton. At the station at about 6:00 p.m., we boarded what was most likely a milk train running ahead of No. 8.

Our train made at least one stop after leaving Binghamton, to pick up a milk car at the state hospital switch. I remember the jerking of the train as it picked up the milk car. In the dimly lit coach I noticed the Erie passenger equipment was dark and dirty.

I vividly remember the hardwood floors of the Susquehanna station as they squeaked and echoed while we walked upstairs to go out the back entrance. We then walked across the small bridge to Front Street. It was snowing and the ground was almost white.

This was our usual way home from Front Street. We went up the walkway and steps, to come out on West Main Street next to John Parrillo's home. Then right up Main Street to the Radicchi home, and left up the hill across Washington Street to Prospect Street.

When we got home, father asked mother to fry the fish (eels). This was a custom for Italians from Moiano; they prepared eel for Christmas Eve dinner. The next morning, Christmas of 1930, the last Mango child was born. Dad named her Pasqualina (Lena), honoring his twin brother Pasquale. When Anna returned to school in January of 1931, the teacher asked her what she got for Christmas, Anna replied a baby sister.

Shortly after that, I entered Barnes Hospital to have my tonsils and adenoids removed. I thought I was going to visit someone there. The only memory I have about that experience is watching another child sitting in her crib cutting cellophane paper. The operation did not help me. Sore throats and ear problems continued for the balance of my childhood.

During the 1920s, my parents had accumulated over $1,000 in a savings account, and were ready to buy a home. They were eyeing an abandoned house one block from the home we were renting on Prospect Street.

In March of 1931, dad bought the home from John Perry for the cash sum of $600. Our new home address was 612 Prospect Street. The only thing I can remember about the move was that after many stops to rest, I managed to carry a wooden kitchen chair from our rented house to our new home.

The two-story house had clapboard siding, originally white but now a dirty gray. A porch went around the front and halfway across the east side. No one had lived there for some time, it had broken windows and the interior walls needed paint.

The first thing dad did was to plant two gardens, one behind the house, and one on the west side of our new home. Then he bought a milk cow, a goat, and several chickens.

Dad was a good railroader and an excellent gardener and farmer, but he was not good at, nor did he like to do general house repairs. During the 1920s and 30s, our neighbors, Mr. and Mrs. John Marshall, helped themselves whenever they wanted tomatoes, lettuce, and corn from dad's garden. In return, the Marshalls repaired the broken windows, papered the walls in the dining room and the parlor, and made the house ready for occupancy. We received much more from them than the combined value of all the garden vegetables over the years. Mother and dad considered them the best of friends and remembered them long after we left Susquehanna.

Prospect Street was a dirt road. When an occasional car went by, it raised a cloud of dust. In the summer, dust got on everything inside and out. Along with the dust, there was the constant soot problem from the steam engines. Even though we lived up the hill four blocks from the tracks, when the wind was right, the smoke reached us.

Our downstairs had a pantry, kitchen, dining room, and a parlor. The parlor had an iron-heating stove in the northeast corner. Above the parlor stove was a vent in the ceiling, the only vent to the upstairs. There was one electrical light in the center of each room operated by a switch inside the room door.

The pump in the pantry worked fine in the summer, however it froze many times in the winter. Mother kept a pan of hot water on the kitchen cook stove to thaw the pump. Sometimes, on very cold winter mornings, even the hot water would not get the pump working.

The second floor of our new home had four bedrooms. The bedroom on the top of the steps was Zi Filippo's room. (We continued to call it "Zi Filippo's room" long after he returned to Italy). We children slept in the room across from his room. To the left, down the hall, was dad and mother's room. An old Victrola was the only item in the room across from theirs, which was always kept closed in the wintertime.

In the summer, or whenever the weather was warm, we spent hours in there playing the few phonograph records we had. Two records we played over and over were dad's favorites, a couple of Sousa marches, and one record of Bezet's opera, *Carmen.* One side of the record was the *Toreador March* and the other side was *Hanbera.*

There was no indoor toilet. We had to go out the kitchen door, down the porch steps, turn left, and walk 40 feet down the yard to get to the outhouse. Outhouses were politely called "back houses." The Italians, pronounced the word as "buckouse." We thought "buckouse" was an Italian word for toilet or bathroom. Later we found many other words that we thought were Italian, were English words that our parents had Italianized.

Many of Susquehanna cellars filled with water during winter and spring, or anytime when there was a lot of rain. We were lucky our cellar remained dry year-round.

One hundred and fifty feet behind, and just to the west of our house, was a big red barn. It had stalls for 6 cows or horses, a large hayloft and an even larger area for the storage of wagons and other farm machinery. That area had items left by the former owner; a hay wagon, plow, and other assorted farm equipment.

By the summer of 1931, I had more courage to leave the immediate confines of our home. I investigated the barn and the hayloft. Getting on the rafters above the hayloft and jumping in the soft hay below was fun. Climbing on and under that old rusted farm machinery was fun for a while, but soon we kids were bored with it.

I remember one spring morning when I heard birds making quite a commotion. As I looked out the front parlor window, I saw a baby bird fly down from the maple tree, hit the railing, and land on the porch floor. I watched with interest for a moment and then something else caught my attention. A minute or so later, mother fried the baby bird in a pan. We ate it, meat and bones, and it was delicious. This was the only time I remember mother cooking, or us eating a baby bird.

One day I went up the path between the VanAken and Woodward house, toward the pasture, a good 500 feet from our home. Near the pasture gate and the woods, in the tall grass, I could smell wild strawberries. I spent quite some time looking for those elusive berries. Mother yelled for me to come home, ending my unsuccessful search.

One very dark night, and it could be very dark since there were no streetlights; I thought it was getting daylight out. I looked outside the parlor window at the empty field, west of the Woodward house, and across the street from the Cooperwaites and Hunts houses, and noticed a big fire. It appeared to light up the night. As I watched it burn I realized the fire was a burning cross, which to me was very impressive. Dad looked out and said, "Non dire mai niente a quella gente" (never say anything to those people). I didn't understand what he was trying to tell me, all I could see was an enormous fire. Adults, I am sure, had no problem seeing the shadows of white-hooded men around that fire.

Years later, when I mentioned this to my sister Marie, she said it was one of several Klan meetings she remembered. My sister, Anna, vividly remembered this particular incident because she was older, and it frightened her. After 1935, I do not remember the Klan. They may have found some other place to have their meetings, or most likely, its few sorry members disbanded altogether.

For the rest of his life, whenever he did not like an individual who was not Italian or Catholic, dad dismissed him as being just another "Ku Kluck."

One bright summer morning, when dad was working in his garden, a very old man came over to say hello. Mr. French's home was on Washington Street; his back yard adjoined our back yard. They talked about the weather and gardens. I was just over 4 years old so I was playing nearby. Mr. French looked at me and promised that next winter he would give me a sled. Next winter for Mr. French never came, because he passed away.

Two of Mr. French's sons worked for the *Susquehanna Transcript* newspaper, and helped publish the first issue. In 1929, Mr. French gave a copy of the first *Transcript*, dated August 2, 1886, to the editor. A fire in 1946 destroyed the *Transcript* and the old *Transcript* editions. These were all of Susquehanna's historical newspaper articles.

Chapter

13 *Giovannina becomes ill*

One winter evening in early 1931, dad was playing with my little sister Giovannina, when he discovered she had an unusual hardness on the right side of her abdomen. The next morning dad took her to Doctor Condon.

The doctor told dad she appeared to have an enlarged spleen, caused by a cold she had at the time. He told dad to wait a couple of weeks and bring her in again. Two weeks later the doctor said he was convinced the cold had settled in her spleen.

Days turned into weeks with no improvement. The doctor finally told dad to take her to a specialist in Binghamton. The specialist read the doctor's letter, asked dad some questions and then examined her. He confirmed that Doctor Condon's diagnosis was correct.

During the next three months to placate dad, Dr. Condon gave him the name of more specialists. Each specialist, who barely looked at Giovannina, read Dr. Condon's diagnosis and agreed with it.

Doctor Condon was the mayor of Susquehanna, as well as the only doctor in town. Dad believed this dual responsibility made him arrogant and full of self-importance, so he was not fully attentive to his patient's problems.

Mother frequently did her "mal occhio" (evil eye) ritual on Giovannina. This was to get rid of any "evil eye" that was making Giovannina sick.

This ritual went as follows: Mother half-filled a soup dish with water, then she took a teaspoon of olive oil and set it beside her on the table. She first dipped her thumb in the olive oil, and made the sign of the cross on Giovannina's forehead. She then held the dish of water over Giovannina's forehead while she said a short prayer that started with "Occhio mal occhio." Then she asked God to stop the "mal occhio" directed toward her little girl. When she finished with the prayer, she poured the rest of the oil in the water. The way the oil spread over the water in the dish indicated if the evil eye directed toward Giovannina was foiled.

Mother remembered when grandmother in Moiano performed the ritual on the first Giovannina six years before, and had two other women in Moiano do the ritual for her. I am sure the ritual made mother and father feel better, at least something was being done for their little girl.

Mother and other women from Moiano performed this ritual, primarily to cure headaches. If someone directed their "mal occhio" toward you, this could cause headaches and or sickness. Because they had many headaches, Marie and Anna were recipients of the "mal occhio" ritual often. Other Italians came to our house for this headache cure, most were women, both young and old.

I remember mother doing her "mal occhio" on me once or twice. It seemed I felt better when she did it. I very rarely had headaches so I am no authority on whether this helped relieve them.

Mother continued to do the ritual all the way through the 1950s. The last time was in 1959, when her grandson, my son Joseph, was 18 months old and had ear problems. Thereafter, for whatever reason, she did not do it anymore. I am sure by then, even she did not believe it had any healing powers.

In August of 1931, Filippo Palma and his family came to visit us. Not our Zi Filippo, but a friend of the family who had migrated from Moiano to Susquehanna. Filippo Palma suggested that dad take Giovannina to his family doctor, an excellent and highly respected doctor in Jersey City. The following week Dad and Giovannina took Erie No. 2 to Jersey City. They stayed at the Palma home that evening.

The next morning, Filippo, Dad, and Giovannina, went to see the doctor. This doctor noted that she had a bad cold, checked the hardness on her side, and asked many questions. He finally had his nurse draw a blood sample and told dad to return with her early that same afternoon. After the doctor examined Giovannina and asked more questions, he advised dad that Giovannina's problem was most likely leukemia. In New York City there were several hospitals and doctors who specialized in childhood leukemia.

However, there was an excellent hospital, the Robert Packer Hospital in Sayre, Pennsylvania, that was much closer for dad. He told dad not to worry; that the other doctors might be right, and the cold may very well be the culprit. He gave dad a letter his nurse had typed, told him to show it to Dr. Condon, and to be sure to give it to the doctors in Sayre. He reiterated, no matter what Doctor Condon said, "Be sure to take Giovannina to the Robert Packer Hospital for a more thorough examination." Dad gratefully thanked the Doctor. He also thanked Filippo Palma for his hospitality, and most of all, for his suggestion of the Jersey City doctor. As they returned to Susquehanna, on Erie No. 27 that evening, he watched his little girl as she slept. He felt relieved that now his little girl would get proper treatment and be cured.

The next morning dad took Giovannina and the letter to Dr. Condon's office. As the doctor read the letter, his face slowly reddened. He knew that in many cases leukemia causes the spleen to enlarge. Why that fact had not entered his mind embarrassed him. He told dad, "Of course I know of the Robert Packer Hospital," and that dad should take Giovannina there. At the Robert Packer Hospital, doctors performed tests on Giovannina for two days. Mother and dad also had blood tests to determine their type. On the third morning the doctor met with dad and mother. He explained about the blood cells in the body, how they work, and what happens to them when a person has leukemia. He went on to say that they knew of no treatment that could cure Giovannina.

Since dad had the same blood type, they would periodically take blood from him for her. This might improve the quality of her life, but only slightly prolong it. It was just a matter of time before Giovannina would die. Dad and mother were distraught over the news; the second child they named Giovannina would die.

The first time mother and dad took Giovannina to the hospital in Sayre; someone had to take care of us. The trouble started when dad suggested they leave us with Zi Pasquale, but Anna refused to go there. Zi Pasquale did not seem to love his two younger boys much less care for any nieces or nephews. He was very mean to us. His cruelty came in subtle ways. One day he asked me, "Vuoi vedere Napoli?" (Do you want to see Naples)? I had heard my parents speak of Naples many times and sure, I wanted to see Naples. He then proceeded to grab both of my ears with his hands and attempted to pick me up. He did not let go until I began pushing him away from me. Anna remembers several similar incidences; she was very vocal in her dislike for him.

Jack, Zi Pasquale's youngest son, was a year or so older than I. He spent many hours at our house during the period when both our families lived in Susquehanna. During frequent phone conversations, before Jack's death in 1991, we discussed the 1930s, our parents, and other related topics. He said his father did not physically abuse he and his older brother Frank, but verbally abused them all their lives. Jack went on to say that everything revolved around his oldest brother, Angelo, and his best interest.

Jack said when his father had one drink he could not stop until the bottle was finished. He was more abusive toward Jack and Frank at these times. Due to this verbal abuse, Jack never got along with his dad. He stayed close to his parents only because of his mother, who treated all her sons equally. Jack did not explain the verbal abuse he received from his dad. However, he did remember an incident when Frank returned home from the Army in the fall of 1945. Frank received a long distance call from a girl, to whom he had been writing, while he was in the service. When his father answered the phone, he hung up on her and did not tell Frank about the call. In order to talk to his girlfriend, Frank had to make the call.

Frank, who served as a sergeant in the Army during World War Two, was not a boy easily intimidated by his father. He told Jack he was leaving Schenectady and would not live near their father again, and he did just that. For the rest of his life he lived in the Baltimore and Philadelphia areas, never close to his father.

Jack's experience gave me some insight of how grandfather Giovanni may have been. As stated earlier in this book, grandfather physically and emotionally abused his younger boys one of whom was Pasquale.

Mother decided to leave Marie, Anna, and Lena with Compare and Comare Radicchi. I knew my cousins, I did not quite know the

Radicchis and I didn't want to be there. Mother reluctantly left me with Zi Pasquale. Luckily for us children, Zi Cesca said that she would watch us in the future. Thereafter, when my parents took Giovannina to Sayre, on every future occasion except one, Zi Cesca took care of us.

Chapter
14 Jobs lost on the Erie Railroad

The effects of the October 1929 stock market crash were now felt locally. The Erie Railroad was not faring very well. Edward Hungerford, in his book wrote, "Erie's total revenues, which reached a high of $129 million in 1929, fell to $73 million in 1932."

The Van Sweringen brothers were dead. All of the dreams of Erie becoming the New York leg of a railroad giant went with the wind. At the Erie's new headquarters in Cleveland, the plans to cut expenses were all too familiar to Erie's management.

The reduction in carloads handled by Erie Railroad, adversely affected some of the most profitable eastbound fast freight trains. Carloads of fruit and vegetables normally made up two eastbound trains, machinery and other manufactured items made up two more. Only two of these money making trains left each day, instead of four.

To help reduce revenue losses, consolidation of the repair facilities was accelerated, along with the elimination of some branch lines and some unprofitable passenger trains. Unused steam engines and rolling stock were taken out of service. All this did little to delay the inevitable; the Erie was back into that too familiar state of bankruptcy.

Job reductions in Susquehanna were beginning to hurt. The consolidation of the engine repair shops in Hornell would soon spell disaster for Susquehanna. The only saving grace was that it took until 1934 before the consolidation was completed, which avoided the immediate and wholesale elimination of the greater majority of the Susquehanna work force.

The only reason for keeping any employees in the Susquehanna roundhouse was to do light repairs on the steam pusher engines. The back shops were converted to repairing passenger and freight equipment. Virtually no rolling equipment repairs were done during the 1930s. Passenger and freight equipment that needed repairs were replaced by equipment that was stored in running order.

The majority of the track gangs throughout the system, composed primarily of Italians ranging in size from 30 to 60 men each, were eliminated. In Susquehanna, 38 trackmen lost their jobs. The track foremen were allowed to continue to work. They could only attempt to keep the systems tracks in good order. Erie tracks were in a state of continuous disrepair during the Great Depression years. It was a bitter pill for the Italians to take. Now that they were approaching middle age, the comfortable style of living they had become accustomed to, was eluding them.

By late 1931, Zi Filippo, with less Erie seniority than most of the other Italians, knew he would soon be unemployed. He had worked for the Erie steadily since he arrived in America. In the fall of 1928, he took time off to return to Italy to marry his childhood sweetheart. Soon after the wedding he returned to America, without his new bride, and went back to work in the roundhouse as a boilermaker helper. Boilermaker helpers, at the time, earned 52¢ an hour for 8 hours a day, 6 days a week. Those who worked in the ash pits earned 49¢ an hour.

Zi Filippo was earning more money than he needed to support his family. After paying his board at our house, and sending enough home to support his wife and a daughter, he still saved half of what he earned. His plan to arrange for his wife and daughter to come to America, and settle permanently, was now on hold.

Reducing the work force in the roundhouse was accelerated. Each time a job was eliminated, the man whose job was eliminated, bumped a person with less seniority. Zi Filippo was bumped from his boilermaker helper job on the 3:00 p.m. shift at the roundhouse. He, in turn, bumped a man with less seniority on the 11:00 p.m. shift. For the next three weeks, each time he was bumped, he went from the night shift in the roundhouse to the day shift at the ash pit. Then the second shift (3:00 to 11:00 p.m.). Finally, he was the youngest at the bottom in seniority.

Shortly before Christmas 1931, a job was eliminated in the roundhouse. The bumping got to him the same day; Zi Filippo was out of work. For a few days he was in a daze; he felt rejected by the country he hoped would "adopt" him. He half-heartedly looked for other work around Susquehanna. However, even before inquiring, he knew there was no work available. Convinced there would not be work for him for some time, he booked passage to Italy, on a ship scheduled to leave New York in late January of 1932.

I do not remember much about the Christmas of 1931. Certainly, it was a sad time for our family. Mother and dad knew Giovannina would not be with us for many more Christmases. Zi Filippo was sympathetic because he knew they would lose another daughter. He tried to cheer up everyone, even though it was not a good Christmas for him either. By the time he was ready to leave for Italy, more Italians and others were laid off, including those who had much more seniority than he had. Any chance he may have had of being recalled got worse each day. By now there were 14 men ahead of him on the roster who were not working, and each day that list was growing.

I knew he was not going to work any more. Each day he went down to the roundhouse to greet those who were still working. Then he would check the notices on the bulletin board. It listed the positions and the date that each would be eliminated. On the day his ship was scheduled to leave for Italy, two more jobs would be eliminated. Nineteen men with more seniority than he had would be out of work.

It was very cold for Zi Filippo's last day in Susquehanna. When he returned from downtown he went up to his room. Twenty or so minutes later he came down carrying two big suitcases, and left them at the bottom of the stairs next to the front door. Mother had made spaghetti sauce with homemade noodles. We had our dinner in the kitchen at the usual time of 5:30 p.m. After dinner we had many visitors, Italian friends from Moiano stopped in to say goodbye to Zi Filippo. Dinner that evening had been quiet. At this late date, I will call that evening the "night of crying." Mother had nursed Lena, which had not satisfied her. Marie tried to give her a bottle and walked with her between the parlor and the dining room to calm her. When Marie tried to put Lena down she cried harder. Sweet sister Giovannina was a month short of her third birthday. I still have a hard time writing her name as Giovannina, because at the time we called her Genevieve. Giovannina in Italian is the feminine of Giovanni (John). Therefore, we should have been calling her Johnna. Why did we call her Genevieve? I remember shortly after she was born in 1929, Mr. and Mrs. Marshall, our neighbors and friends, stopped by to see the new family addition. When Mrs. Marshall asked dad what the new baby's name was, dad replied, "We nama her 'Ge o von neen na,'" as the Italian pronunciation sounded in English. Mrs. Marshall replied "Genevieve. I like that name, and she is a very cute little girl." She looked over at Marie, Anna, myself and said, "I bet you like your new sister Genevieve."

Giovannina was also crying, Mother took her into the kitchen where the adults were, but she began to cry harder. Mother carried her back to the parlor and put her on the couch where she seemed to calm down a little. Nevertheless, she continued to cry. One of the visitors that night was Zi Giovanni Oropallo. With him were his sons. Carl was my age; Billy was older than I. Zi Giovanni, due to the railroad accident mentioned in an earlier chapter, had chronic emphysema. As a little boy it bothered me because, when he spoke, he had to pause between words to take another breath. I liked him and felt much respect for him. When Zi Giovanni walked he threw his left foot in and was a little bow-legged. Many of those from Moiano were given nicknames by their peers, usually for obvious reasons. Many of the nicknames were lovingly given. Others were downright mean. They called Zi Giovanni, "Giovanni coscia storta" (Crooked leg John).

The visiting children and I clowned around to try to make Giovannina laugh. She just sat on the couch and cried. Occasionally our clowning would be funny to her and she stopped crying momentarily to smile, but just as quickly she continued to cry. Most of the visitors brought cakes and cookies. We ran into the kitchen to get a treat off the table, which we offered Giovannina. She had eaten very little at the dinner table and did not take anything we offered.

During the evening, my parents, Zi Filippo, and each guest, came in to talk to her. She remained on the couch crying softly. I really do not remember much of my little sister. I do have that picture of her sitting on that couch and crying, and more than just that one time. She probably endured much pain and cried to relieve her suffering. The chore of washing the dinner dishes fell directly into Anna's hands. Mother put the dishes into a pan of hot water in the sink. Anna had to stand on a box in front of the sink to reach the dishpan. After washing each dish she had to rinse it off by pumping water from the pump, which was hard work for a 7 year old. Worse than that, the temperature outside was about 25 degrees; the water coming from the well was ice cold.

Anna cried softly as she struggled to get the job done. Whenever Lena quieted down, Marie would come in and with one arm around Lena, she used the other hand to pump the water for Anna. Every time Anna thought she was almost done, mother brought in more dirty dishes. To Anna's delight, Zi Toro and Zi Cesca arrived. When Zi Cesca saw Anna in the pantry she chased her into the parlor, and 15 minutes later Zi Cesca had all the dishes washed. Anna stood near the parlor stove to warm up and continued to cry for a few minutes. Soon, she was doing her best to entertain Giovannina, just like the rest of us.

Eventually we gave up trying to make Giovannina laugh. Lena fell asleep, Marie, Anna, and Billy, started to calm Giovannina. I liked Billy Oropallo and looked up to him. As a little boy, if I could have chosen a big brother, it would have been one of my cousins, Angelo, Frank, or Billy. Billy began to ask me to repeat words. When he said, "Johnny say river," Giovannina smiled even before I answered. Of course I let him know that I could; I repeated "wiver." "Say railroad" Billy said, Giovannina smiled again, and I repeated "wailwoad." Then he asked me to say arithmetic, Giovannina laughed out loud. The adults were happy and relieved that Billy succeeded in easing Giovannina's pain, even if only for just a short while.

For the next 30 minutes Giovannina was content to sit on the couch and watch us. She occasionally smiled at our antics. Soon her eyelids were too heavy for her to keep open, and she gradually fell asleep. One of the last visitors that evening was Mrs. Catalano. Everyone in the kitchen was in tears. She had been married to Carmen Antonio Oropallo, but she had remarried. Dad and Zi Filippo remembered how good a friend Carmen Antonio was, when they were children in Italy. Their final memory of Carmen Antonio was of him under the steam engine, scalded by the escaping steam, which caused his death three years earlier.

Mother's eyes were moist all evening; her brother was returning home to Italy. She would not have him to comfort her anymore. She had her big brother around all her life. She also knew that he might never return to America. She remembered when they were kids at home. He would tell her, "scopa il pavimento" (sweep the floor). She would reply, "Tu non sei mio capo" (you are not my boss). Some times he would then sweep the floor, but most of the time she ended up sweeping it.

In 1925, he was in America to comfort her when she returned from Italy after the first Giovannina had died. Now, six years later, she could not imagine having gone through that period without her big brother's comfort and strength.

Shortly after everyone left, it was time for me to go to bed. Zi Filippo hugged me and, as he said goodbye, he put 50¢ in my hands. Wow, I thought! I was rich! I did not realize I would never see my Zi Filippo again. I went to bed and put the 50¢ under my pillow, and then I quickly fell asleep. Many evenings when Zi Filippo returned from work he brought me a Hershey chocolate bar. Mother would never again wake me up at 11:30 p.m. to give me Zi Filippo's present.

At 10:30 p.m. it was time to leave for the station. Zi Filippo also gave Marie and Anna 50¢ when they went to bed. He put 50¢ next to Lena, and a dollar bill next to Giovannina. Both were asleep on the couch. He bid mother farewell and said, "Non piangere cara sorella mia, sono sicuro che ritornero in due anni" (Do not cry my dear sister, I am sure I will return in two years).

Dad, who was working the 11:00 p.m. shift at the roundhouse, had gotten permission to arrive a little late that evening. He picked up one of the suitcases and headed for the station with Zi Filippo. As they walked down the hill to the station, they discussed America and how good it was to everyone, and how the world was changing. Airplanes were not only transporting mail, but people too. Lindbergh's New York to Paris flight, less than five years before, took only 33 and one-half hours. In comparison, the fastest ships took 6 days from New York to LeHarve, and 16 days from New York to Naples. Some Italian families now had automobiles. The distance from Susquehanna to Binghamton was 30 minutes by automobile. It used to take them four hours to walk the same distance from Moiano to Naples. Dad said that when he came to America in 1913, he had to wait over a year before the Erie hired him. He told Filippo he was sure that they would soon be calling those laid-off to return to work, in which case, he would quickly notify him by transatlantic cable. The conversation went to their childhood, early in the century and how hard times were in Moiano. Even in Italy things had gotten better. Mussolini seemed to be doing a lot for Italy. Moiano now had electricity. Dad wondered what it was like in Moiano at night with streetlights.

At the station, Zi Filippo checked his two suitcases in the baggage room and put the check receipts in his wallet. As they walked to the waiting room, dad handed him two ten-dollar bills with instructions to give one to both of their fathers, Giovanni Mango and Giovanni Palma. While seated in the warm waiting room, Filippo remarked that had he been smart enough to come to America with dad, Carmen Antonio, and Giovanni Pepe in 1913, he would have enough seniority and would still be working. And that maybe his wife and daughter would now be in America too. This return home may not have been necessary.

A few minutes later they could hear two short toots of a distance steam whistle; number 10 was leaving the coal pockets. They walked out on the station platform as a westbound fast freight train was slowed to a stop on the mainline. The engine pulling the freight was a new Erie 3300.

No.10 came around the curve pulled by one of the new 2900 passenger engines. This was the first night that No. 10 was powered by one of those. Ironically engine 3116, (The same engine Carmen Antonio got scalded by steam in March of 1928) was in front of No.10, and being used as a helper engine for the run up to Gulf Summit.

Filippo looked down the platform until he saw the baggage man put his two suitcases into the baggage car. He hugged dad; they tearfully bid each other farewell. When he boarded he sat on the south side of the coach so he could wave goodbye to dad. As No.10 headed east, at 11:20 and on time, Filippo waved a final good-bye to dad as he watched him hurry down the track to the roundhouse. Filippo got a last look at downtown Susquehanna. A car that had just come across the river bridge and through the railroad underpass turned on Main Street and headed toward West Hill. The Model A Ford stopped under a streetlight with steam erupting from the engine. The hood was up with the owner standing in front surveying the problem.

Filippo thought that car headed for West Hill could be back on Prospect Street in four minutes. So close, but suddenly Prospect Street, his sister Maddalena, her family, his time in Susquehanna, already seemed far away. He had a deep feeling that he would never see the Erie, Susquehanna or America again. He had experienced much pain in his joints the last three weeks, and was happy that in Italy he would be free of that pain. He was thankful he had come to America; he had accumulated a small fortune over the last ten years. He remembered when his father came home from America thirty years ago and how well off they were, and how fast his dad's American savings were spent.

He peered out the window when the train stopped in Gulf Summit. The 3116, helper engine uncoupled and went in the siding to let No 10 pass. He looked back at the pusher enveloped in a cloud of steam. A quick glance up in the engine cab showed that the firebox door was open. He could see the deep red glow and the silhouette of the fireman, as he shoveled coal into the fire. Filippo tried to sleep, the sadness of losing his job and the excitement of returning home was too much. It was lightly snowing, and the ground was white as the train made stops at Deposit, Hancock, and Callicoon. The snow sparkled from the reflection of the few lights in each town. When they left each station he could feel the surge of power of that new 2900 engine as it pulled the train. No.10 would have no trouble keeping to its schedule this night.

After Port Jervis, there were bigger stations and more lights to see in each town as the train neared Jersey City. It was no longer snowing, and a light drizzle began fogging the windows of the train. Before arriving in Jersey City at 5:00 a.m., he devoured the two meatball sandwiches Maddalena had prepared for him. Jersey City was cold and damp. He patiently waited for his luggage in the baggage room, and then headed down the wooden platform to board the Chamber Street ferry.

The ferry ride across the Hudson was made uncomfortable by the cold, damp wind. The predawn view of the New York skyline was impressive, and he would not soon forget it. He was not sure if he'd ever view it again. It was not easy to carry his luggage and walk six city blocks along the waterfront to the pier where his ship was docked. Other passengers were already inside the covered pier. He felt warm, out of the sharp cold wind, as he sat on his luggage waiting patiently for the ships gangplank to be lowered. After boarding the ship, he found his cabin where he left his luggage. He then went back up on deck to get a last view of New York City as the ship headed down the Hudson River. He paid special attention to Ellis Island, and looked carefully at the large brick building and the docks where immigrants used to wait for the boats to take them to The Battery. No boats were at their pier, even though it was after 11:00 a.m. He could see no one at the pier or on the walkway to the pier. Ellis Island appeared deserted. Zi Filippo went back to his cabin with renewed excitement. When he got off the ship in 16 days, he would be in Naples, and only a couple of hours from his hometown.

Zi Filippo never returned to America. Even though I have not seen him since that night those many years ago, he remained my favorite uncle. He raised four children, two boys and two girls. Two of his older children, John and Maria, came to America in 1950 and settled here permanently. He outlived all of those who had immigrated to America. He quietly passed away in Moiano, in early February of 1993, seven months short of his ninety-eighth birthday. He was one of the last Italians to return to Italy from Susquehanna. The Italian community was now stable and permanent. Many children of the Italians in Susquehanna were adults and married. There were now three generations of Italians in town. Italians immigrating to America started slowly in the 1870s. The new restrictive immigration laws enacted during the 1920s virtually shut the door on Italian immigration to America. Due to the severity of the Great Depression an immigrant of Italian, or of any other ancestry, would have no job waiting for him. The streets of America were no longer paved with gold.

Chapter

15 *Misfortunes*

At 2:00, on a very cold Sunday morning, February 21, 1932, mother woke us to look out the window toward downtown. We could see a red glow that silhouetted the trees and houses. Mother said Zi Pasquale's house was on fire. Zi Pasquale was working the night shift at the ash pit when a fellow worker told him his house was on fire.

With great fear and apprehension he headed for home. He tracked the flames in the sky even before he could see his house. His fast walk turned to a run. He gingerly stepped his way through a moving westbound freight that was slowly heading west on the main line. He was just west of the back shops when he saw his house. As he came up the bank onto Main Street, near Mike Pagano's store, he could see flames in the window upstairs. As he ran up Main Street toward his house, he was crying and praying at the same time. He asked God to save his family, his wife Rose, and his boys, Angelo, Frank, and Jack. When he was closer he saw the fire truck, which had just arrived and had the hoses ready to pour water on the flames.

He knew no one could survive such a blaze. He told God that he took good care of his family, and asked why He would take them away from him. He didn't know Rose had awakened from coughing due to the smoke. She ran to the boys' room where she picked up Jack, dragged Frank off the bed to the floor, and yelled at Angelo to wake up. With Jack in her arms and holding Frank by the hand, she pushed Angelo ahead of her down the stairs. In thirty seconds they were downstairs and out the front door.

They were all coughing and had a hard time catching their breath as they ran down the concrete steps to the sidewalk. Rose looked up and was surprised to see how quickly the second floor was flaming. As she was thanking God for guiding her and the boys out safely, she turned and saw her husband as he ran toward them. He had not seen her yet, and now many of the neighbors were there, and the fire truck had arrived. Before she realized how cold it was, a neighbor came with blankets for each of them. She wore only her nightgown and the boys had light pajamas. Rose tearfully thanked the neighbor for being so helpful, so quickly, at that time of night.

Pasquale arrived out of breath, with tears running down his face. He was angry because he didn't see anyone trying to rescue his family from the burning building. He headed up the concrete steps from the sidewalk, determined to enter the house and save his family no matter what. Ten feet from the house he heard shouting. He turned his head and saw Rose and the boys. His relief was enormous and he thanked God for sparing them.

The following Tuesday morning February 23rd, dad and mother were scheduled to take Giovannina back to the Sayre hospital where Giovannina would receive blood transfusions. Because Zi Pasquale and family were living with us after the fire, mother didn't have to worry about the rest of us children.

That morning after work, Zi Pasquale found a house for rent on Jackson Avenue, which already had a stove and some furniture. He returned to our house, where he slept for a few hours. When he awoke, Marie had already returned from school. He asked if she could take care of us kids. Marie replied that she could. Zi Pasquale and his family headed for their new rented house. Down on the east end of Washington Street, Benny Bucci, owner of Bucci's Grocery Store, was surprised when Pasquale Mango and family came in to patronize his store. For three years Pasquale had lived two blocks down on West Main Street, and he never once stepped foot in his store. We were fortunate that 11 year-old Marie was so mature. She stayed home from school and prepared meals and snacks for the next two days. Lena, just over one year old, needed much attention. She kept clean diapers on her, prepared her bottles, and kept her warm and fed. She also dressed Anna warmly and sent her off to school. Most importantly, she kept the fire going in both the parlor and kitchen stoves.

When mother, dad, and Giovannina, returned Thursday afternoon, February 25th, they asked where Zi Pasquale and his family were. Marie replied that they left Tuesday afternoon. Mother was so furious she could be heard down on Washington Street. She told dad, "We will soon lose another daughter! What if our house had burned down? We would have returned home and found that we had lost our other four children. Your brother's house burned down just five nights ago. The temperature outside at night has not gotten any warmer."

" Marie had to keep fires going in both the parlor and kitchen stoves. Your brother had to keep two fires going in their house and it burned down. In that house the mother was home. He was not concerned that the same thing could have happened at our house, and with no adult there." "How could he leave four little children at home alone in the middle of the winter? Would you do that to his family?" Dad was embarrassed and upset that his brother was so unconcerned for us. He knew he would never leave any children home alone, no matter what the weather conditions were. Nevertheless, he did not say anything.

That evening Zi Cesca and Zi Toro came up to see how Giovannina was. They were both surprised and very upset at what Zi Pasquale had done. Zi Pasquale knew that Zi Cesca would have gladly come up and taken care of us kids. She said that had he told her, she would have quickly come up to our house.

Zi Cesca and Zi Toro lived on West Main Street. Had Zi Pasquale and his family walked down West Main St., the Italians would have seen them and told Zi Cesca, who would have immediately come up to our house. When Zi Toro visited us in the wintertime he would usually sit on the kitchen floor, next to the cellar door. He sported a mustache and many winter evenings when he came by we could see ice crystals on it. He expected a glass of wine from mother and, even though Zi Cesca did not want mother to give him wine, he always got it. He was a happy person, he never gossiped and he seemed to like everybody. He liked us kids and we liked him. We listened intently to any stories he had to tell. When he heard about Zi Pasquale, he developed a particular dislike for him, and from that time on called him "Trippa di Vermi" (belly of worms).

I remember Zi Cesca, when she came up to take care of us, during mother, dad, and Giovannina's trips to Sayre. She sat all night on the old rocking chair in our kitchen. She took care of us as well as mother did. Zi Cesca and Zi Toro had more than their share of misfortune. They lost two infant girls due to the flu; an ailment that took many lives young and old during World War One. In the 1920s they lost two sons to other illnesses. Zi Cesca remembered that when she lost the infant girls my father, still a teenager was there to help. When she lost the boys both dad and mother were at her house to help anyway they could.

One Sunday, during the 1920's, Zi Cesca boiled a large pot of water, which was needed to remove the feathers from the chicken she had just killed. Veronica, her daughter, remembers this accident: She and Billy were playing with a roll of string in the parlor. Zi Cesca put the pot of boiling water on the floor, ready to dip the chicken into it to remove the feathers. At just that moment four year-old Billy backed into the kitchen and fell into the hot water. For many weeks it appeared Billy would not live. Zi Cesca did not go to bed to sleep; she slept sitting in a chair in her kitchen for one full year. Fortunately, Billy got better and is still alive today. Zi Toro and Zi Cesca's difficulties during the early part of the 20th century would fill more than another book.

Zi Toro, six weeks before the Zi Pasquale fiasco, had come up to our house to feed his cow, shortly after a big snowstorm. He occasionally left his cow in our barn when there was so much snow. There was an old toboggan, a turn of the century model, in our barn, which had been left by the Perry family. Marie had been eyeing it since we had moved there and had waited for just such a snowstorm. She took the old toboggan and both she and Anna were having a great time riding it down our side yard. When Zi Toro came up to feed his cow Marie asked, "Zi Toro, vuoi andare con noi in coppa della slitta" (Do you want to ride with us on the sled)? Zi Toro, very young at heart, replied, "Si."

The toboggan was big and had enough room for the three of them. Marie sat in front to steer, although no steering was necessary because it was a straight run 200 feet down the yard. Anna sat in the middle and Zi Toro sat in the back. As they started down the yard Zi Toro's eyes focused on two vertical barn slats that had been badly damaged, probably by the toboggan and they were headed straight for the barn. Looking out the dining room window as the toboggan whizzed by, mother began to laugh as she realized Zi Toro's predicament. The speeding toboggan was halfway down the yard when Zi Toro realized that these two crazy girls could not stop until the toboggan crashed into the barn. He quickly put his feet down to stop. The toboggan failed to stop; he slid off the rear. He didn't stop either, but continued to roll down the yard. Snow flew all around him as he dug his arms and legs into the snow to slow his descent. He lightly hit the barn sideways, right next to where the toboggan and the girls had hit it. Zi Toro's mustache and hair were packed with snow. Marie collected his hat, dusted the snow off and handed it to him. He dusted himself off, went into the barn and did his chores.

Mother was still laughing when Zi Toro came into the kitchen. He said, "Quelle guaglielle avrebbero potuto uccidere il loro caro zi" (Those girls could have gotten their dear uncle killed). Mother replied, "Avreste potuto sapere meglio di andare sulla slitta con due piccole guaglielle" (You should have known better than to get on that sled with two little girls). Regardless, a glass of wine later, Zi Toro was no worse for the wear.

Chapter
16 *Settling in Our New Home*

In the spring of 1932, the city of Susquehanna brought water and sewer lines through our end of Prospect Street. After those trenches were filled, a tar and gravel machine paved our street. This eliminated the dirt road and most of the dust problems.

Albert Woodward, an Englishman who was our neighbor, helped dad partition one corner of a bedroom. They installed pipes and water lines, and soon we had a bathroom with a big cast iron tub and a toilet. We never had to go to the backhouse again. The old bedpan was discarded and at last, we were beginning to enter the 20th century. A sink with hot and cold running water replaced the well pump in the pantry. Before that, water was heated on the cast iron stove in the kitchen. The trauma of the frozen pump on winter mornings was suddenly only a memory. The well and the water pump in the yard remained; it still provided us with clear, cold water in the summer.

During those years we had a piano in our dining room. I do not know when my dad got it. Marie played quite a few tunes and was quite good for not ever having taken lessons. Anna was even better, she just sat on the piano stool and played anything she wanted. I can still hear Anna playing "*Scatter Brain*," a popular song of the day that was Anna's favorite. In later years dad paid for Lena to take lessons, and she became quite adept at playing many classical and popular tunes. The piano was part of our home through the end of World War Two. I loved to listen to my sisters play. It was also a player piano. It had two or three player rolls. All you needed to do was to insert one of the rolls, fold down the wooden foot pedals that sat over the piano regular pedals. Pumping with your feet started the piano roll turning and the piano playing. I did not know any of the music on those rolls, nevertheless I occasionally found myself playing them. As a very small child, I learned to play the first 8 or 10 bars of the *Star-Spangled Banner* with one finger. Years later, about the time I graduated high school, I could play the first 8 or 10 bars of the National Anthem with two fingers.

During the 1930s and early 1940s, the piano provided much entertainment in our home. On selected evenings and holidays the family gathered around that piano. As Marie, Anna, or Lena played, we all sang the words. Unfortunately, the piano is not as common in today's homes.

I especially remember the first time I went to Sunday mass at St. John's Catholic Church with Marie and Anna. We walked into the church, which looked cavernous to me. Three-quarters of the way down, it had what appeared to be a white fence, and behind that fence stood a man dressed in white. I thought, "Could it be," so I reached over to my sister Marie and tugged at her dress. I said to her, "Is that God?" Marie turned, looked down at me and said, "Shut up." It was a long walk from our home on Prospect Street to church. On winter Sunday mornings, we stopped in the heated post office downtown, about halfway there. It was a welcome respite on our way to and from Sunday mass.

My memories of Susquehanna, during the 1930s, and during the depression, are many. Some are good and some are not so good. We went to the Washington Street School close to our house. The school, built in 1889, was constructed of brick and had two classrooms downstairs and two upstairs. They were quite large with high ceilings. When you entered the front door there was a hall and steps. Downstairs, the door on the right was the first and second grade room. The door to the left was the third and fourth grade. Upstairs, to the right, were the fifth and sixth grade. I do not remember the room on the left being used. The building basement housed an old steam furnace. Classrooms heated by steam were quite comfortable, even on the coldest winter days. Each classroom outside wall had very large windows and on most days, they provided all the light required for a teacher to conduct her class. There were three teachers for 6 grades. Gertrude Murphy was the first and second grade teacher, and probably was married. She was in her 30s. Catherine Ryan was the third and fourth grade teacher. She had to be in her 20s, because she later married one of the Radicchi brothers. The fifth and sixth grade teacher was Mrs. Lanning. To me, she seemed to be very old, probably close to age 60. I later found out why her gray hair always seemed to be styled the same. Mrs. Lanning was later promoted to Principal. Anna Coyle, who seemed middle aged, neither young nor old, became the fifth and sixth grade teacher.

I remember my first day of school in early September of 1933. Mother dressed me in a new pair of knee-length knickers and stockings, and a new pair of black high-top shoes. Those new knickers were patched and re-patched. I wore them well into the third grade. My sister, Anna, walked me to school. Because the teachers were having their morning coffee, we children were required to walk down to Washington Street and wait on the corner, one-half block west of the school. Children coming from east of the school waited on the corner, one-half block east of the school. Soon a teacher came out the front door, walked down the concrete school steps to the first concrete landing before the sidewalk, where she swung a hand-held bell. This was a signal for all of us to then walk the remaining half block to school. We waited on that corner for the teacher to swing that bell no matter what the weather was like. When we went in the school door, Anna pointed to the classroom on the right. I remember Frankie Cannini, who sat two rows away from me. We fashioned a ball out of a piece of clay. He rolled it to me and I rolled it back until the teacher stopped our fun.

I remember many times during my grammar school years of a rhyme that spoke about me and other students who might have a hole in his pants. "I see London, I see France, I see a hole in Jimmy's pants."

Some of the very poor kids came to school in blue jean overalls. I used to feel sorry for them, but then my worn out knickers were no better.

The first three months of school were traumatic for me. Giovannina, who was very sick and dying, took all of mother's time. Other than that first morning, I had to fend for myself. Most mornings, mother was still upstairs with Giovannina, and I had to get up on time and dress myself. Marie couldn't help me. She left for school earlier because she started the seventh grade at Susquehanna's high school. When we went downstairs in the morning, we would yell up to mother and ask her what there was for breakfast. She would answer, "Fa zuppa." This meant to get a piece of her homemade bread, soak it in a glass of milk and eat it. I never liked bread much, including her homemade bread because a few hours after it came out of the oven, it became very hard.

Many mornings I went without breakfast. I had to wait on the cold street corner until some idiot teacher came out to swing the bell. I came down with one cold after another. Each time it settled in my ears. Earaches as a child, was the worst pain I experienced all my life. By November, one or the other of my ears was infected for the rest of the winter. I had a continuous runny nose. I must have been quite a sight, because in class, I probably dried my runny nose with my shirtsleeve.

Along with my runny nose and earache I had developed a toothache. It was an early December day, two weeks before Giovannina died. On the second day of the toothache, I came home from school crying. Apparently mother told me to go downtown to the dentist. I had never gone to see a dentist, but I knew where one was because I had seen a sign on a door that read "dentist." I headed downtown, went into the door, and up the stairs to his office.

The dentist set me in the chair and asked me which tooth hurts? I pointed to the baby molar. He said, "that doesn't look like a tooth that could have pain." He asked me to point to it again. He put his finger on it and said, "are you sure this is the one?" I hadn't noticed that he had anything in his hand, but as I answered yes, he reached in with forceps and pulled the tooth out. I cried going down the steps and out on the street on my way back home, as I held a small piece of gauze to stop the bleeding.

Trouble from a dentist wasn't enough. The next morning at school the janitor stopped in the lower classrooms and advised each teacher that someone was writing on the boy's room wall. Apparently Mrs. Murphy already had a bad morning. She quickly surveyed the class to determine just who the culprit might be. To my misfortune she decided that I, a first grader, was the guilty one. I had just walked in the room and was sitting down at my desk. She came over to me and grabbed me by the ear that was tender and hurting due to a current ear infection. I was not quite sure where she wanted to take me as she pulled, the pain was excruciating. We went across the classroom, down the hall, and into the boy's room.

In the boys room she shouted at me, "Why did you write on the wall?" as she pointed to the wall above the urinal. I couldn't reach as high as some of the words were. I also couldn't read many of the words on that wall. She had to know after seeing the wall that no first grader wrote it. I cried as I answered that I did not write on the wall. Nevertheless, still tugging me by the ear, she walked me back to my seat. Fortunately, for the rest of that school year the teacher left me alone. She promoted me to the second grade and then to the third grade. Looking back to those days in Susquehanna, for me to be promoted two years in a row was a miracle. This was not the only such incident. Unfortunately, there were several other sorry experiences.

The teachers at Washington Street School had good jobs that paid well. With their salary, they could buy good food, clothing, and entertainment for themselves. To the contrary, most of their students' parents had no steady work. The parents struggled just to provide food and shelter for their children. No matter how much love the children received at home, it still wasn't easy for them. Countless other students had unhappy experiences at the hands of those four teachers. Many of my fellow students shared my exact feeling. One student, who later became a dentist, always remembered and talked about the inadequate performance of those who called themselves teachers in the Washington Street School. I also do not have any respect for the teachers who treated us so cruelly.

Catholic children attended catechism class one afternoon a week after regular classes ended. We had to go to Laurel Hill Academy, the Catholic school for Catholic instruction. That fall, six year-old children received instructions to prepare for their first Holy Communion. Laurel Hill Academy religious classes lasted throughout the 1930s. What was important for me, and unlike the Washington Street School, the nuns treated me like just another student. I came to class each week with the weekly assignment completed. I remember one assignment, the nun said we must memorize the "Apostles Creed," and we must have it memorized for class next week. I thought I could never memorize it because it had so many big words. I went home that night, and before I went to bed, I had it memorized. Each evening, for the rest of that week, I made sure I had not forgotten it. In class the following week only three students had it memorized. I was the only one of the three, with no coaching from the nun, who said the "Apostles Creed" without hesitation.

Those days were mostly happy; we had very little in material things, but neither did anyone else. Because of the large garden, a milk cow, chickens, and occasionally a pig or goat, we had enough to eat.

Mother canned tomatoes, beans, and corn, made Italian cheese, baked bread twice a week, and on rare occasions, she churned butter. The few groceries we needed were bought at Mike Pagano's store on the bottom of Main Street, or Benny Bucci's store on Washington Street. Dad occasionally gave us kids a penny. After getting the penny we quickly ran down to Condon's Grocery Store, on West Main Street, because it was the closest store. With a penny we could purchase a licorice stick, a large wad of bubble gum, or other assorted candies. I am amazed at the patience that Mr. and Mrs. Condon had while we decided which piece of candy we wanted. When it was very hot in the summer dad occasionally gave us a nickel. We immediately headed for the Sugar Bowl downtown. Five cents bought an ice cream cone with three dips of ice cream, and each dip could be a different flavor if we wanted.

The only opportunity I had during those years to earn any money was in the winter when it snowed several inches. I used to ask our next-door neighbor, Mrs. Ahearn, if she wanted her sidewalk shoveled. Most of the time she would tell me to go ahead. I happily obliged because when I was done she paid me 5¢. Mrs. Ahearn was a quiet neighbor and seldom came out of her house. Her older son lived with her, and to my knowledge he never left the house. She said he was gassed during World War One. In later years we found out he was also an alcoholic.

The number of Americans unemployed increased since the stock market crash three years earlier. Most large cities across the country had bread lines and soup kitchens. Many men in those cities carried signs that proclaimed that they would do anything for pay to support their families. In Susquehanna no one carried signs. Everyone knew that the only place that work might be available was the Erie. The Erie, however, was not hiring.

In March of 1933, Franklin Roosevelt became our new president. In his first year in office he proposed and passed much legislation to help the country out of The Depression. The despair of the country turned to new hope that this president might get us out of those dark days. Many who may have been Republican before The Depression now were Democrats. The closure of the banks by Roosevelt in early 1933 did not affect our family. Due to Giovannina's leukemia, dad had used what little savings he had in the First National Bank, Susquehanna's only bank.

Soon we began to hear of the different national programs Roosevelt and congress passed to help us out of The Depression. The Works Progress Administration (WPA) was one. I do not remember many WPA jobs in Susquehanna. The National Rehabilitation Administration, or the National Recovery Act (NRA), made government loans to businesses. The Civilian Conservation Corps (CCC) was an organization some of the young men in town joined. Most of the CCC camps were in the western states. It was good, clean living for those who joined. The CCC repaired roads, planted trees on public land, improved our national parks. All these programs made the 30s a decade of initials. WPA, NRA, and CCC, everyone knew them by initial only. In the end, all of Roosevelt's legislation did nothing to end The Great Depression.

During that period, a new man took over the government of Germany. He was small in stature, with a mustache similar to one worn by a popular silent film comedian named Charlie Chaplin. This Austrian born paperhanger by profession was not a comedian. Hitler, with his gang of Nazi accomplices wearing brown shirts, black and red armbands displaying a crooked cross (swastika), were seducing the German people. The world did not seem to care, nor take seriously, what he had written in his book *"Mein Kampf,"* of the superiority of the Aryan German, and the inferiority of Jews and other non-Aryan people.

The depression in Germany did not last very long. The armaments industries started building tanks and airplanes. Hitler was preparing Germany for the conquest of Europe and the world.

No story of Susquehanna and the Great Depression can be told without recounting the wreck of Erie passenger train No. 8, Tuesday, September 5, 1933. I vividly remember that evening; we were in the kitchen, the kitchen light was off, and mother had a candle on the table. We had to be very quiet because dad, who was a light sleeper, was sleeping. He had to work the 11:00 p.m. shift. There was a knock on our front door. John Marshall came up to tell us of the wreck.

That evening No. 8, with eight cars, left Binghamton headed for Jersey City two minutes late at 7:14. It stopped at the red signal, a little over a mile east of the BD interlocking plant (tower). BD tower was located about a mile east of the passenger station. The signal was red because, just ahead at the state hospital switch, the switch engine was switching the milk car that was to be added to the milk train (running as Third No. 2), about 3 minutes behind No. 8. As the milk train approached BD tower its signal was red over yellow, which indicated there was traffic in the block ahead. The rulebook required the milk train to stop and then proceed at 15 miles per hour.

After leaving BD tower in the twilight of this early September evening, engineer Shea of the milk train could see between the trees and brush. The signal for the next block (where No. 8 was coming to a stop) was red. Again, among the trees and brush, Shea could see the signal east of the state hospital switch, almost three miles east of his position was green. He mistakenly assumed that No. 8 was gone and it was the switch engine getting the milk car ready for his train to pick up. The milk train engine 2928, consisting of 17 milk cars, rounded the curve going over 30 miles per hour. When Shea saw the rear of No. 8 stopped, he applied the air brakes, but his train slammed into the rear of No. 8. The rulebook required that a switch engine conductor ask permission from the train dispatcher to use a main track outside of yard limits. I am sure he had permission, normally the train dispatcher would have told the switch engine conductor to let No. 8 pass first. I could not find from the newspaper article any evidence that the switch engine conductor did not have permission from the dispatcher to use the eastbound main track ahead of No. 8. Nevertheless, had engineer Shea of the milk train, been following the rules, the accident would not have occurred.

No. 8's rear car was a parlor car just ahead of it was a coach. Both were made of steel. Just ahead of that was a very old coach made of wood; the rest of the train cars were made of steel. The wooden coach took the full force of the impact. The steel coach ahead of the parlor car telescoped 14 feet into the wooden coach. The majority of the passengers in the wooden coach were Susquehanna residents who were returning from Binghamton. Ten of the 14 passengers who were dead, and ten of the 25 injured, were from Susquehanna. Eli VanAken, Erie Delaware divisions train dispatcher, died of shock and internal injuries. His wife Mildred, who sat next to him, fractured her leg in several places. She survived, but she wore a leg brace for the rest of her life. Needless to say that over the next week, Susquehanna was in mourning. Almost everyone in town knew someone who had died or was injured in the wreck.

Chapter

17 *The final Days of Giovannina*

Dad worked off and on during the last half of 1933. I remember watching him coming up the street from work, and just by the way he swung his lunch bucket, I could tell he had been laid off again. We cannot know what was on his mind, he was aware he soon would be permanently laid-off, and another of his little girls would die. Before the years end, he would lose both in that order.

I am sure he again thought that God had abandoned him as he had thought when he was a child and his mother died. The Sayre Hospital doctors told dad in late October, that it was futile to bring Giovannina in any more. However, early in the second week of December, when Giovannina could barely walk and against their advice, dad decided to take her there again. He hoped another transfusion might help her. Anna went with them on the last visit to the Sayre hospital. This is what she said of that last trip: "The Sayre doctors were saddened when they saw how weak Giovannina had gotten. They smiled and joked with me, and remarked how alert and pretty I was. They told dad that the transfusion would not help Giovannina, and at the same time it would weaken him. Dad had to do one last thing for his very sick little girl. He insisted that the doctor give her his blood this one last time." Anna said; "they were in a cold hospital room. Dad sat on one hospital gurney and Giovannina was on another one. Tubes were connected between them, and very soon, she could see the red blood running in those tubes. After the transfusion, the doctor took dad aside and told him that Giovannina would not live longer than two weeks."

Late December 1933 was extremely cold. The fires in the kitchen and parlor stoves were kept going at full strength. We could hear the wood and coal crackle as they burned. To mother this was an omen. She had heard this crackling when her father tried to keep their home extra warm, when the first Giovannina was dying of the measles, during the unusually cool August nights in Moiano, eight years earlier. I especially remember the severe cold weather. Our home was kept as warm as possible. The inside of the windows were completely frosted. By placing your hand for 30 or 40 seconds on the center of the window, you could temporarily defrost a large enough area to look out.

On Christmas Eve 1933, Giovannina told mother and dad, "Mi sento la morte per tutto mio corpo" (I can feel death all over my body). The day after Christmas, as Giovannina was failing rapidly, dad asked Dr. Condon to come up and treat her. The doctor knew he could not do anything for her, but he could not deny dad this one last effort for a dying child. Doctor Condon came later that afternoon, and went through the motion of checking her heart as she lay on the parlor couch. He felt so sorry for her that he reached in his pocket and placed a quarter in her hand. Giovannina was so weakened that she could not close her hand to hold the coin.

When I went to bed that night, mother with tears running down her cheek, was "Facendo il mal occhio" for Giovannina one last time. Very early the next morning, December 27, 1933, our dear sister died peacefully in her sleep. The trauma of the last three years had ended for mother and dad, and our whole family. That morning Zi Pasquale and Zi Rosa (who remembered dad had spent three days at their house when little Anthony died four years before) were at our house before we children were awake. Dad carried Giovannina's body to the mortuary for embalming. Zi Pasquale, as diplomatically as possible, and in his broken English, took each one of us aside as we came downstairs that morning.

When I woke up, I heard Mother, Marie, and Anna crying. I came down the steps and went into the parlor. Anna was behind the parlor stove crying, Mother and Marie wept together at the dining room table. Zi Pasquale called me aside and said, "Johnny, U little sister, Giovannina, passa away lasta night, God tooka her to heaven witha Heem." I started crying even before Zi Pasquale finished what he was saying. No one can know how traumatic this is to a small child. The more mature the child, the greater is the loneliness they feel, and the longer it lasts. Zi Pasquale and Zi Rosa remained at our house for two days to help as much as they could.

Later that day (I do not remember them bringing it in), in our dining room, was the casket with Giovannina lying in it. She had one hand on top of the other, holding rosary beads. Giovannina looked very peaceful. Around the casket there were many carnations. Anna said due to that experience, she still can't stand the smell of carnations. After the initial shock, I was numb. I knew they would soon bury my little sister and I would never see her again. At three years old, Lena was too young to fully comprehend her sister's death. For the next two days our home was full with visiting relatives and friends. It was customary for everyone who came to bring food. Whenever I was hungry I went into the kitchen to choose among a variety of foods on the table. For the most part I just sat in a chair in the dining room or on the couch in the parlor.

On the third morning, December 30, the temperature outside was below zero. After a short funeral mass at St. John's Catholic Church, the procession went to the cemetery. The burial site was next to our cousin Anthony's grave. All of us kids were shivering. It seemed the ceremony would never end. We watched as the casket was slowly lowered into the ground. I vividly remember the topography of the gravesite where Giovannina was buried. Thirty or forty square feet of the grave area had a gentle even slope to it. In 1945, when I returned to Susquehanna, the first place I went was to the cemetery to see my little sister's grave. In the summer of 1989, when my wife Pia and I, traveled to Susquehanna, we visited Giovannina's grave. All those years we had referred to her as Genevieve. It was at this time that I came to realize that Giovannina was not Genevieve in English. On her gravestone, her name is spelled Jiovanina with a J instead of a G, and one n was left out. Dad, I am sure, told the person who carved the name on her gravestone that the first letter was G. However, saying G in Italian could sound much like a J in English. I am also sure that when he saw the stone weeks after Giovannina's death, he was too nice to complain to the person who carved the name incorrectly on the stone.

During our visit I noticed that Giovannina's headstone leaned to the right. I spent one afternoon with a pail, water, and mortar, and hardly any tools to fix it. This corrected much of the leaning of the head stone. Since I had mixed too much water in the mortar, I had to wait more than an hour before I could finish the job. I spent some time walking around the cemetery reading other tombstones. Some friends I knew long ago are buried in that cemetery. I felt an inner contentment just seeing those tombstones, and thinking of each deceased person.

Chapter
18 *Food Supplies during The Great Depression*

It was quiet in our house for the rest of the 1933-1934 winter. In memory of our little sister, dad did not allow the radio to be turned on for one full year. Thereafter, to keep the electric bill low, the radio was turned on very little. The food supply improved; our cow had a calf the fall of 1933, and the following spring she was ready to milk. With two cows producing milk, mother decided to sell milk to some of our neighbors. Each evening she sterilized four or five quart-size milk bottles needed the next day. Early the next morning, before school, Marie delivered the milk to our customers. Mother also made cheese and sold it. Apparently the local dairy did not like to lose the four or five customers taken away from them. One cool morning, two men, dressed in suits and ties, came to our door. Claiming they were from the health department, they told mother she was not complying with health department rules. They said she didn't have the proper sterilization equipment, so she was not allowed to sell milk

On cool days mother hung flat, round wicker containers on our side porch, each held about one pound of curing cheese. The men asked mother what they were. When mother used to tell this story she said she wanted to tell them "non e fara tuo" (it's none of your business). Mother reluctantly told them it was cheese. They did not ask if she sold cheese too. Mother discontinued selling milk. Thereafter, she sold more cheese.

During those years we had many farm animals. Shortly after we moved to the house on Prospect Street, dad purchased a goat. Goat milk is very creamy and it was used to make cheese. Cheese made from goat milk was strong and very tasty. The goat was worth feeding just for the cheese. One day the goat stopped producing milk. Dad then decided to butcher it for the meat. Dad, who was a gentle man, could never kill any animal. Zi Toro was asked to kill it and he did so. Zi Toro had the goat in the barn, with a sledgehammer in his hand. Just at that moment I decided to look through a crack in the door. One blow with the sledgehammer on the goat's head and Zi Toro killed it. Seeing this at five years of age, I ran in the house and told mother that Zi Toro killed the goat and could also kill a man if he wanted. This tickled Zi Toro. We shared the goat meat with Zi Toro's family, the Marshall's, and Mrs. VanAken. Mother continued to make cheese, with cow's milk, throughout the rest of The Great Depression.

A better story was the piglet dad had purchased. It was kept in the barn with the cows. When closed, I could squeeze through the barn door without opening it. Two or three days later the piglet squeezed through it, and dad caught a glimpse of it crossing the street and heading for the woods. He yelled at Anna to catch it. Anna took off after it across the field toward the woods. Before she realized, she was alone in the woods and the piglet was nowhere to be seen. Being alone in the woods made Anna afraid. She retreated back out across the field and home. Dad was just as happy to lose the piglet because he was beginning to be attached to that little beast. Besides, when it was time, how could he have it butchered?

Three mornings later, dad went into the barn to milk the cows. Dirty and somewhat thinner, the piglet was waiting to be fed. Mother said, "Dio sapeva che era comprata con moneta stendate." Roughly translated, "purchase of the piglet was with money earned from hard work, God would not let us lose it." The only thing I did not like about the piglet was that dad planted two long rows of potatoes when he knew he was going to purchase a pig. That fall it was my job to dig them. I worked very hard one week after school, making little progress, when dad decided to finish the job. We stored several bushels of potatoes in our cellar. That winter, Mother mixed the potatoes with other food scraps for our pig. The following summer we had a fat and very healthy pig.

A man, who specialized in that work, butchered our pig. He received one-third of the meat for his labors. Our family spent the next two weeks making Italian pork and blood sausages. For a long time we had ham hocks, pigs feet, pork steak, pork ribs, or fresh ham for dinner. That pig fed our family as well as neighbors and friends for many, many days thereafter. We were happy to eat almost anything in those years. Dad occasionally went to the meat market downtown and purchased a cow or pig's head. Mother boiled the head for a couple of hours in a large pan. At the dinner table we all cut off a favorite piece of meat. On the cow's head, I especially liked the eyes. I would dig into the eye socket with a fork, until the eye came out. It was very tasty.

I liked springtime the most because dad planted scarola (escarole) and rapa. Before the rapa plant flowered, mother would cut the buds with the leaves around them. "Broccoli di rapa" was then boiled, prepared with garlic, olive oil, and salt. The rapa plant grew wild and during April and May, mother and dad picked them in any vacant field on West Hill. Another wild green vegetable that mother called "orecchielle" (little ears) was my favorite. The whole plant was cut at root level, then boiled and prepared with salt, garlic, and olive oil. Of course dandelion was another wild vegetable that was in abundance in the spring. A "frittata di orecchielle," was my favorite. To make this, you take a plate of cooked orecchielle, add two eggs, mix well, season and fry in low heat for about five minutes.

In the summers, up in the pasture where the cows were left during the day, there was an abundance of huckleberries, blackberries, and raspberries. We picked them to eat fresh and mother canned both huckleberries and blackberries. Many people in town came up to help themselves, there seemed to be enough berries for anyone who spent the time to pick them.

I loved it when mother made ricotta cheese, because she then made lasagna or ravioli. The ravioli were shaped in a half circle the straight sides were 3 to 4 inches in width. Each had plenty of ricotta in them, and three of them made a very tasty meal.

Along with the depression the mid-western states had a drought. Farmers accustomed to plenty of rain now saw their farmland turn to sand and dust. Great dust storms covered parts of Kansas, Oklahoma, and Missouri. Many farmers, who might have survived the depression, lost their farms to the drought.

In Susquehanna there was plenty of rain; the summer crops of vegetables, corn and tomatoes, were abundant. There was plenty to eat for our family, and the many other families in town who had gardens, raised chickens and other farm animals. Mother and us kids worked the hardest during canning season. It started when the first tomatoes ripened in late July.

My job was to carry all the empty glass jars up from the cellar. Then each jar was cleaned. Mother would send me downtown to Mike Pagano's store to buy new rubber washers. They went between the glass cover and the jar to seal the can properly. The tomatoes were cleaned, cut, and each jar was filled with tomatoes. The rubber washers were then placed, the glass cover was put on top and the metal snap was secured. The jars were then placed in a big kettle and boiled for an hour or two. This was a long and hot job, because the kitchen wood stove was kept going in spite of the summer heat. Each summer mother canned 100 jars of tomatoes this way.

Canning beans and corn was equally difficult. Along with all this canning, mother canned about 25 jars of tomato paste. This was harder yet! The tomatoes were first boiled; they then were peeled and strained through a thin wire mesh colander, extracting just the puree. The puree was then cooked down to a paste. The jars were filled to the top with this paste, sealed and boiled. In our home there was no rest until the last jar was placed on the shelf in the cellar.

Dad also worked hard all summer. Early each morning, he had to milk and feed the cows and feed the chickens, and do his usual gardening chores. Each day he sharpened the sickle he used to cut grass, and I had to turn the whetstone for him, a job I hated. Then he was off to a vacant field with his sickle to cut the tall grass. Later, when the hay dried, he used the wheelbarrow to bring it to the barn and place it in the hayloft. He did this all summer to get enough hay for the winter.

Even though we lived four blocks up the hill from the railroad, our home was still found by railroad bums and they would knock on our door. When Mother saw them outside the parlor window, she quickly identified the knocker as being a bum. Years after the depression we found that everyone else in America called them hobos. Mother never let them into the house, but in her broken English she told them to wait. She then went in the kitchen and fried two or three eggs and served them with a large piece of her hard Italian bread. The bums quickly consumed the meal and profusely thanked mother for her hospitality.

One cold day, dad was home and got into a conversation with one bum, who had a jacket and no hat. Dad had one hat with earmuffs. Dad gave it to the bum as he was leaving. Mother hollered, "Come hai fatto a regalare l'unico cappello?" (How could you give him your only hat)? Dad's reply was that, "Occorre piu a lui che a me" (He needs it more than I do).

Chapter
19 *Another Christmas*

Marie worked at many odd jobs from the time she was 6 years old. Dad had purchased an old Singer sewing machine for her. She made dresses for herself and others. She also set women's hair and cleaned floors for some of our older neighbors. Most of her money went for purchasing groceries. At Christmas time in 1934, she had managed to save 85¢. For most Christmases, my sisters and I went up to the woods across the pasture from our house, and cut down a pine tree. It usually was too big for the house and had to be trimmed considerably. The tree was then carried into the parlor and placed in the coal pail. We filled the pail around the tree trunk with coal and added some water. The coal held up the tree and the water provided some moisture to keep it fresh. From our unused room upstairs, we brought down the old cardboard box full of ornaments, tinsel, and one string of lights, to decorate our tree.

It was the day before Christmas. Marie remembered that the year before we had missed Christmas because Giovannina died. She knew that if she did not do something about it, we would again miss Christmas. With the 85¢ in her little purse, she put on a heavy sweater, overcoat, and galoshes over her shoes to go downtown. It was one of those days when there were heavy snow squalls that lasted three or four minutes. It snowed so hard you could hardly see, and the snow stuck to everything. Prospect Street looked like a Christmas picture card. Marie was white with snow when she walked into the warm and comfortable Ryan and Alpaugh Variety Store, Susquehanna's five and ten. Her first stop was at the record counter; three 78RPM Christmas records were on sale for 98¢. She looked for popular music records. One she especially liked, popular at the time, was "*Paper Moon.*" She flipped through the records and mentally picked two others she might have purchased if she had the money.

A small Victrola, which cost $3.99, was kept running by the clerk at the record counter, who played selected Christmas songs. When one record ended, the clerk cranked the Victrola then put another one on to play. One of Marie's teenage friends had a Victrola just like that one in her bedroom. Marie dreamed of having her own room with one of those Victrolas, and a collection of her favorite records. She looked at all the items in the store, including candies that were inexpensive. She looked at the toys marked "Made in Japan." Most of these were wind up toys. Although the prices were right, she knew that Japanese toys were very flimsy and broke very easily. She did not want to spend her money on things that would not last.

Marie took her time as she went up and down the store aisles. After each purchase she calculated how much more she had left to spend. For me, she bought a 10¢ coloring book on Africa, and a small 5¢ box of crayons. For Anna, a school tablet with a picture of Santa Claus across the whole cover, and a package of three pencils for 15¢. For Lena, she bought three cut out dolls with six cut out dresses; for 10¢. She bought a long wooden spoon for mother for 10¢. For 5¢, she bought dad a key ring; hanging by a small chain from the ring was a miniature replica of a steam engine. After she bought all our presents she had enough left to buy a package of 12 small candy canes for 10¢. With another dime she bought wrapping paper and string, enough to wrap and tie all the presents. She checked her purse before she left the store to make sure she still had 10¢ left.

As I looked out the kitchen window at the heavy snow squall, I was impressed when I saw Marie, white with snow, carrying a bag as she walked up the sidewalk. She came in the front door instead of the kitchen door, and went upstairs with her bag of presents. Nobody paid any attention to her. Nor did any of us think to look under the bed where she hid the wrapped presents. We did not look anywhere else for hidden presents; none were expected this Christmas. We were sure this man called Santa Claus, whose picture adorned some of the store windows downtown, would not be stopping at 612 Prospect Street this year.

Marie was the first to get up that Christmas morning. She quietly retrieved the presents from under the bed and carried them downstairs. She placed them under the tree and she hung the candy canes on the tree branches. But when we woke up, we went straight to the kitchen; no one bothered to look in the parlor at our sparsely decorated tree.

In Moiano, on Christmas morning when our parents were children, children would find an orange or apple as a gift. As children we expected, and got the same, from our parents. On this Christmas morning, as with other holiday mornings, mother made cepolas, by mixing a dough similar to bread dough, but very soft. She placed a small handful in the frying pan and deep-fried them. When they were done, mother rolled them in sugar. We stuffed ourselves with the delicious hot, sweet cepolas.

Marie placed an extra large cepola in the center of the table. Mother made it for Lena because it was her fourth birthday. We all sang happy birthday as mother cut pieces of the cepola for each of us. Lena smiled when dad gave her a pair of knitted gloves for her birthday. I was eating my piece of the birthday cepola with a glass of milk. Anna was peeling her orange, which dad had bought for each of us. Lena was eating cepola with a fork, because she would not take her gloves off.

Marie then called all of us into the parlor. We were all so surprised; there under our Christmas tree, with candy canes hanging from the branches, were presents from Marie. We unwrapped them with joy. Mother was happy with the wooden spoon, she needed a long one to stir the homemade tomato sauce, or for summer canning projects. Lena, with her new gloves still on, got out the scissors to try and cut out her paper dolls' dresses. Anna proudly was writing in her tablet. Dad smiled as he cut the old shoelace that held his three keys together. Now he could place the keys on his new key ring. I was so busy with my coloring book; I had not noticed that there was only one thing wrong this very, merry Christmas day. Marie had no present under that tree. Oh, how I remember with love and with great fondness my sister Marie!

Marie, Anna, and I, went to St. John's Church 9:00 a.m. Christmas morning mass. We sat in the usual pew, near the left rear of the church. After saying an "Our Father," Marie walked down the church aisle, and on the opposite side of the altar where the votive stand was, she put that last 10¢ in the coin slot. Her final gift was to light a candle in remembrance of our dear deceased little sister Giovannina.

That same afternoon, Lena's Godmother, Comare Mollicca, and her daughter Mary, came to our house. She brought Lena a doll and carriage. The doll, covered with a blanket in the carriage, almost looked like a real baby. When I was a child I always had wanted a wagon. I never asked for one because wagons cost maybe, as much as three or four dollars. Any money our family had was used to purchase food. That much money for a toy was out of the question.

A year or two later I got an idea. Four wheels and a board would make a wagon. Francis McGee, down the street, had made a wagon with the help of his dad. It worked fine. He could steer it with a rope attached to the front axle. I found a board about 16 inches wide and three feet long, and four spikes, which dad had taken from somewhere else and had straightened out for future use. I went to Lena, since she was not playing with her doll carriage very much anymore, and asked if I could have the wheels. Lena, who always had a good heart, would have given me the doll and the whole carriage had I asked for it. I nailed the wheels with those spikes on all four corners of the board. I had made a very crude wagon very quickly. It would hardly go downhill without being pushed. The wheels angled outward because the spikes were not strong enough to support the wheels with weight on my crude wagon. When we moved from Susquehanna, the crude wagon, along with the rusted carriage minus wheels, were left under our porch.

Another Christmas, when I was in the fourth grade, I announced to everyone that I wanted a pocket watch just like dads'. I said it so often that I believed I really would get one. How do you tell an eight year old that he is not going to get a pocket watch for Christmas? I must have touched everyone's heart. I was not surprised on Christmas morning, when I not only got one watch, but three of them. Dad, Marie and Mrs. VanAken, God bless them, had each purchased a watch for me. A pocket watch cost 98¢, a lot of money during those Great Depression years. The watches dad and Marie, purchased were, of course, returned.

I had my watch and it became the best Christmas I ever had, up to that time. I took my watch to school with me every day. Very frequently I took it out of my pocket and wound it. One day it stopped and would not run any more. When I got home from school, I told Marie that it had stopped running. She proceeded to unscrew the back of the watch to see what was wrong. As the back came off, it seemed to explode. The spring, which was wound too tightly, just popped out of the case. I did not get another watch until my Confirmation, when I was 13.

Chapter
20 *Discipline and Education*

One cold winter afternoon, dad gave me a fifty-cent piece to take to Mr. Cooperwaite, who lived 300 feet west of us on Prospect Street. I felt very proud that dad asked me to do something so important. I put on my jacket, went out the front door with the coin loosely held in my left hand, and ran to the Cooperwaite house.

About 40 feet from our house I realized that the coin was no longer in my hand. I went back home and carefully told Dad that I had lost the 50¢. He did not scold me. He went out to where I said I might have lost it. I watched him until it became dark. He sifted one shovel of snow at a time through the coal ash sifter. I do not remember if he ever found that coin, but I do remember the value of money, especially during those lean times. Dad, although he did not scold me at that time, was nevertheless very strict and consistent with his discipline. He left no question in our minds as to correct and incorrect behavior. I always tried very hard to behave, especially when dad was around. I can remember only a handful of times while growing up when he actually hit me.

Mother was another story. When we misbehaved and she became angry enough, she might come after us with the broom. In the summer, I would run outside and stay away from her for one-half of an hour or so, until she cooled off. However, if mother said she was going to tell dad, this always got my attention. We never dared to run away from dad, we stood there and took our punishment. During those times, as children of Italian immigrants, we could not go home and admit that we were punished at school. In fact, a child told his friends not to say anything at home when their parents were in hearing range. If the parents learned of any misdeeds at school, the perpetrator would receive additional punishment at home.

One example of this in those times, told to me by Pat Parrillo, was about his little brother Louie Parrillo, who went to the Catholic elementary school (Laurel Hills Academy). One day Louie came home and told his father that the nun had slapped him on the face. Lou's father replied, "Da quale parte della faccia ti ha battuta?" (On which side of your face did she hit you)? As Lou pointed to his left cheek, his father hauled off and slapped him on his right cheek.

A fortunate incident at the Washington Street School resolved a big problem for all Italian kids, the year before I started school. It is the story of the fifth and sixth grade teacher Mrs. Lanning, and her propensity for punishing Italian students. Throughout the 1920s and early 1930s, when she decided a student was not learning their lesson well enough, she called the student to the front of the room. She asked a question and told her victim to write the answer on the blackboard. Any hesitation, especially by an Italian student, caused her to grab the student by the hair and pound the student's head on the blackboard. Italian students had a lot of hair so this made Lanning's method of punishment easy for her.

Billy Oropallo, as I noted before, was a very bright kid, and at 10 years of age, he decided he did not want his head pounded against that blackboard. Early in the school year of 1932, Lanning told him to write his answer on the blackboard. While he began to consider the right answer, she grabbed him by the hair. Billy quickly decided he would do the same to her, but when he grabbed her hair it came off. Seeing their teacher standing there, virtually bald-headed, the students in the very tense classroom burst out laughing. Mrs. Lanning did not think this was funny at all. She was very embarrassed that they not only knew she wore a wig, but that they knew she was bald. She immediately expelled Billy from school. Billy suffered great anxiety on his way home. He didn't know how to tell his father that he got in trouble at school. Had he not been expelled, nothing would have been said and the whole incident would have been forgotten.

The attitude of Italian parents was that if you got into trouble with a teacher, it was your fault. Thus, you got more punishment at home. Billy had no choice; he had to tell his father that he was expelled from school. Billy's father (Crooked-leg John) immediately headed for the Washington Street School. When he confronted Mrs. Lanning she ordered him out of her classroom. The Italians, who had children attending Washington Street school, knew of Lanning's readiness to pull hair and pound their heads against the blackboard. They also knew she concentrated on Italian boys and girls. They did not like her manners and most of all, both Billy's father and the other Italians did not want Billy expelled from school. An immediate and special meeting of the Sons of Italy was called. The lodge members asked Giuseppe Radicchi, the lodge president, to be their spokesperson. They then arranged a meeting with the school board and Mrs. Lanning.

· What went on during a very long school board meeting is very sketchy. We know that Billy was allowed to return to school. And from that day forward, Mrs. Lanning did not lay a hand on any of her students. All the Italians kids who later attended the Washington Street School, including myself, had Billy to thank. Billy, who I do not think was ever formally thanked, barely passed his 60th birthday when he died in the early 1980s.

I spent half of my fifth grade year in that school. Former teacher Mrs. Lanning was now the principal; my teacher was Mrs. Coyle. They displayed a heavy ruler, but to my knowledge it was not used, at least not while I was in that class.

Another good thing that came out of that meeting was the promise by Mrs. Lanning that she would soon eliminate the practice of students having to wait on the cold street corner in the morning. However, it was over two years later when the teachers decided to have their coffee in the vacant room upstairs. We always walked into an empty classroom each morning until the teachers' coffee time was over

By June of 1936, I was in the fourth grade. Our class was taking the final test for the year. The test was to determine if a student could advance to the fifth grade. I sat in the row farthest from the windows, on the fourth grade side of the classroom, and about five seats from the front. Just in front of me was a girl. I will call her Helen. Our teacher Miss Ryan warned us, that if she caught anyone copying another person's paper, she would fail that student and the student would have to repeat the fourth grade. I had just begun to answer the first question on the test when Helen turned around just for a second and looked at me. I was too busy reading the next question to pay any attention to what Helen was doing. A few seconds later Helen turned again and briefly looked at me; she could not have copied anything because she had not looked at my paper long enough. In both instances neither one of us spoke.

Suddenly, Miss Ryan was standing next to us; she took our papers, and just that quickly, we both knew we had to repeat the fourth grade. We were made to sit in that class while the rest of the students completed their tests. I was devastated and embarrassed when I had to go home and tell my parents and sisters that I did not pass. Helen did not deserve to fail the fourth grade just for turning briefly twice to look back at my exam paper. Miss Ryan had to know she could not have copied anything. I was not happy that I was failed when I had done nothing wrong. Today I am glad that I was made to repeat the fourth grade. Had I not, I would not have had an excellent experience with a superior teacher in the sixth grade in another school. Furthermore, I was able to make up that lost year in high school.

I remember at about age 10, on a cold winter day, after school was out, a friend and I were going to Catholic instruction. On West Main Street, just up the hill near Mike Pagano's store, a couple of bums said hello to us. They couldn't have been more than five or six years older than us. I still remember to this day the hungry, desperate expressions on their young faces. I felt inadequate because there was nothing I could do to help them. We said hello to them as we continued to walk to Catholic instruction. Two or three days later we heard that the two, who apparently were brothers, were found in an empty boxcar frozen to death.

When Lena was a small child she talked to anyone who went by our house. After I started school, and Giovannina had died, mother was home alone with Lena. On warm days she let Lena go outside. When someone walked by the house, Lena would strike up a conversation and then follow the person down the street. Mother soon tired of chasing after her. One day when I came home from school, I could see mother had solved the problem. Lena was tied around the waist with an old clothesline, the other end tied to the porch post. Lena was not concerned; she could still talk to anyone going by.

We had all of the childhood diseases, the measles, mumps, and whooping cough. Dad would stop at Doctor Condon's office to tell him when we were sick. Before the end of the day the doctor would visit us. He verified the particular disease and told mother to keep us warm and in the house. The following morning we would hear pounding on our front door. Some official person was designated to post notices on doors of every house where a family member had a contagious disease. The card was about a foot square, and I know it had the words, "notice," "herein," and "contagious disease." Just exactly how it was worded was never any part of my memory.

Chapter
21 Memories of the 1930s

Another view of Susquehanna during the depths of The Great Depression, was written by my schoolmate Dorothy (Lake) Holmes. She replied to an article in the *Susquehanna Transcript*, in the Lou Parrillo column, "News Beat." Parrillo wrote, "No doubt, many of our new senior citizens will remember the Pasquale Mango family. His children attended Laurel Hill Academy. Mr. Mango, age 94, could well be one of the last members of all the Italian immigrants who came to Susquehanna in the early 1900s to work on the Erie Railroad."

"While talking to Mr. Mango, although not as agile as he used to be or would like to be, his mind is just as sharp as could be. We talked of many other Italian families, long gone from the community and many happenings that took place." Dorothy's response to the News Beat article was entitled "West Hill Memories." The *Transcript* printed it on Friday, August 5, 1988. She wrote: "Our recent article about Patsy Mango was a heart-warming story to me as it brought back a lot of happy childhood memories. I was a child of the 1930s living on Prospect Street and a neighbor of the Joe Mango Family."

"One special memory was of sitting on the porch of the Joe Mango household, which was later the Paul and Gladys McGuane home, with the Mango children, Johnny, Anna, and Marie, listening to Mr. Mango playing the accordion. I remember the death of their daughter, although I was real young at the time."

"The early days of the 1930s were hard times, depression times. I remember anxiously waiting for the cold bottles of milk to be delivered to our door, as it must have been a government sponsored program for the needy as it wasn't often we had it. The homemade clothes that we wore were made by the Ladies Sewing project in Oakland, state sponsored to give women jobs. Also the W. P. A., for men who maintained our streets in town, the CCC's government jobs for young men of the neighborhood to put them to work in the summer time, all under F. D. R.'s administration."

"In Washington Street School there were 6 grades. Gertrude Murphy taught first and second grades, third and fourth by Catherine Ryan, Fifth and sixth by Anna Coyle. To buy an extra school tablet we had to cross the street to Sidney Hurley's home. A beautiful red covered tablet cost only 10¢ and a pencil for 5¢; unheard of today."

"Getting sprayed by the fire hydrants on a hot summer day on Washington Street, picking blackberries in the pasture on Prospect Street, following Salvatore Mauro as he brought his cow Pulomel (butter cup) up the hill from West Main Street to the pasture every day. We children loved him."

"Receiving a bag of candy for us kids when mom paid the bill each week at Zenobio's grocery store was our big treat! Who could forget Jackie Hurley with his big booming voice crying 'ice,' as he peddled his wares up and down the hills, us kids following him, hoping for a big chip of ice to suck on during a hot summer day."

"Harry Darling, a full blooded Indian who liked to fish in the river, brought us a large carp one time. Mike Dean, Chief of Police, lived on Prospect Street, you could see him all times of day riding up and down the hills on his motorcycle that had a sidecar, going about his duties."

"We kids played ball in the street, there was not much traffic in those days, but just hoped the ball didn't go into the Fred Hoyt's yard as he would keep it. Ha! These are just a few of the precious childhood memories about growing up in the 30s on West Hill."

I remember sitting on our porch on warm summer evenings. The sound of the railroad was never far away. We could hear the trains ten miles across the valley. The slow chug, chug, chug, of the steam engines as they labored to push eastbound freight trains up the hill to the summit was a familiar sound. The lonesome steam engine whistle conjured thoughts of some far away place unknown to us. Today the sound of a train brings back those memories.

I remember the old iceboxes that were not very good. To get ice delivery, mother placed a sign in our parlor window. One side up it read 25, when it was turned around on the same side it read 50. The iceman then knew that we wanted delivery of ice, and whether we wanted 25 or 50 pound piece. Occasionally, especially on a hot day, we chipped off a piece of ice and ate it.

I remember listening to my Dad play his accordion. Whenever and wherever Dad decided to play we all listened and enjoyed his little concerts. Dad could play any song on the accordion if he knew the melody.

I remember the meat wagon pulled by an old horse, which occasionally came up to Prospect Street. I still remember the delicious smell of hot-dogs. It was a treat when mother bought a hot dog for me, or when mother made meatballs and I would steal a raw piece of ground beef.

I remember mother on Mondays, with a scrub board and bar of brown wash soap. Kneeling next to a large tub half-full of water and dirty clothes, she scrubbed clothes most of the day. After the clothes were clean, the dirty water was replaced with clean water to rinse them. A hand-operated roller attached to the washtub removed most of the water before she hung them on the clothesline. On Tuesday, she ironed clothes. The two irons she had were heated on the kitchen stove. When one iron cooled she placed it on the stove, then took the heated one to continue her work.

It was about the middle 1930s, when Dad purchased a second-hand electric washing machine. Washing clothes became easier, although mother still used the scrub board for extra dirty items before she put them in the washing machine.

Susquehanna had one theater called The Town Theater. Every Wednesday afternoon they had children's matinee. The price for a ticket was 10¢. I never asked mother for money because I knew our family could not afford it. Spaulding Bread Company included a coupon in each loaf of bread. With 12 coupons, you could see a free show any Wednesday. Saving 12 bread coupons was quite a feat when your mother made bread. Our neighbors Mrs. Ahearn, or Mrs. VanAken, quite often had a couple of those coupons. In two or three weeks, I might have as many as six coupons saved. We kids soon found out that when we had six of them, and we folded one or two of them so that it looked like the stack contained more than the six coupons, the collector at the theater door would let us in. God bless those guys, a child could always get in with 5 or 6 coupons, and we were not fooling anyone.

Mother occasionally gave me some change and told me to go down and get a haircut. I guess the barbers knew I wouldn't have enough money but they gave me a haircut anyway. When they were done, I would give them the change mother had given me, the total might be 25 or 30¢. Posted in the shop were their fees, adult haircuts 75¢, children 50¢.

I remember when mother finally decided to apply to become a citizen. She was given two sheets of paper with statistical information on our government. The applicant needed to know the answer to 12-15 questions. Mother spent many days studying the material. At the hearing the judge asked each applicant three or four of the questions.

Giuseppe Radicchi, and one other Italian, always accompanied Italians to the court in Montrose, where citizenship hearings where held. Mother answered the first three questions quickly. On the fourth, "how many sitting judges on the Supreme Court?" she hesitated. Giuseppe, or the other person trying to help, whispered under his breath "Dici sette" (say seven). Mother very proudly told us kids that even though she was given the wrong answer to the question, she correctly answered "nine." Her citizenship certificate was proudly hung on the wall in our parlor.

In 1934, we received two Trans-Atlantic cables from Italy. The first came in September from Zi Lillo, advising Dad of his father's death. Dad was a very gentle man who was easily moved to tears. But that was the only time when I actually heard him cry. The second cable we received was from mother's brother, Zi Nicole, advising of her father's death on December 13, 1934. Mother, who had been treated like a queen by her Dad, cried for a whole day. This sad news came during a Christmas season.

At age seven, the death of my grandfathers had no effect on me. Grandfathers and grandmothers were only individuals in photographs on our parlor wall. We, the new American-born Italians, did not experience the love and affection of grandparents. The older generation in Italy could not see their American grandchildren. They could not relive the memories of when their children were just babies, or experience the pleasure of seeing grandchildren grow up. There is forever a void in the life of each generation: the old one in Italy, and the new one in America.

Chapter 22 *Summertime*

Summertime on Prospect Street was quiet. Cousin Jack, Zi Pasquale's youngest son, who was close to my age, and the closest I had to a brother, came up to our house most days. We did things that any 7-9 year old boys did at the time, like playing checkers, tag, and baseball. In the summer Marie made Kool-Aid for us with cool water pumped from our well. Jack remembers that as our glass emptied we would run down to the well to add more water to the Kool-Aid. Soon we were drinking just plain water. When Jack's older brothers, Angelo and Frank, came to our house they usually persuaded Marie to make fudge, and that was always a special treat for all of us.

In the summer of 1935, Angelo, Frank, and Jack, along with Marie, Anna, Lena, and myself, told our parents we wanted to have a picnic up on the Indian Rocks. Indian Rocks were large pieces of broken bedrock exposed above ground in the pasture. They were exposed probably due to erosion of the soil over the centuries. Some were as much as 6 feet or more above ground. Most likely Angelo, or Marie, the oldest in each family, started the request. Times were tough. Dad and Zi Pasquale had not worked for almost two years. Even though they had other things to worry about, the picnic was scheduled. Mother prepared spaghetti and meat balls for everyone. We all went up the pasture carrying the food and utensils, picked a special secluded Indian Rock in the woods, and all had a great time.

Jack and I spent much time together until 1936, when Zi Pasquale announced they were moving to Schenectady, New York. Father James Welch, at St. John's Church, missed Angelo and Frank, because they had been altar boys. Each year the American Legion gave out two awards for academic achievement, one to a boy, and one to a girl. My cousin Angelo received that award at Laurel Hill Academy in the eighth grade that year. I have always marveled at how intelligent my three cousins were. We missed them after they left. I, of course, especially missed Jack. The day before they left, Jack came up to our house and asked Marie to wave his hair. He had heard that in Schenectady, boys had wavy hair. I didn't remember to ask Jack later in life, what happened when he showed up on Manhattan Street in Schenectady, when all the tough Italian kids saw him for the first time.

In the 1936 national election, Alf Landon ran against Franklin D. Roosevelt, and of course there were also local elections. A candidate for the post of Commissioner of Highways and Streets asked dad if he would stand near the polling place on Election Day, and ask all Italians voting, to vote for him. He told dad that if he won, he would get him work when the Highway Department needed an occasional extra man.

Miracle of miracles, dad's candidate won. For the next year and a half, as the winning candidate, he kept his promise. I remember the excitement in our home. When there was a knock on the front door early in the morning, we knew a person had come up to advise dad to report to work that day.

One summer evening young Paul McGuane Jr. called me to come across the street. His dad's (Mrs. VanAken's son-in-law Paul Sr.) car was parked with the trunk opened. Young junior showed me a large dead snake in the trunk. Paul Sr. apparently had run it over on a local road somewhere around Susquehanna.

My parents and Zi Cesca had gone up to the pasture to fetch the cows. When they went by with the cows, Paul Sr. had the snake on the ground. While standing over it he told them he had just killed it. Paul Sr. was somewhat of an alcoholic. I did not like him when he occasionally came up on Prospect Street while intoxicated. Thereafter, I had no respect at all for him, because I knew he had lied about where the snake was killed.

One other summer evening we came home and found our cow had gotten out of the pasture. She was in Mrs. VanAken's garden eating her corn. Mother went up and led the cow to our barn for the night. Mrs. VanAken was not home, however the next day she discovered what had happened. She came down to mother and said "Salvatore's (Zi Toro's) God damned cow got out and ate some of my corn." Mother did not respond to her accusation. However, two or three weeks later when our corn ripened, Dad had me take a bushel of large ears to Mrs. VanAken. No more was said of Zi Toro's cow eating Mrs. VanAken's corn.

Zi Toro loved wine. Zi Cesca kept reins on him because she felt he occasionally drank too much. One day Zi Toro came up to mother and asked, "mi potrebbe prestare una pesta?" (Could you lend me a dollar)? Mother said he did not have to borrow a dollar, and she happily gave him one knowing full well why he wanted the money.

At home he hid his stash of wine in the cellar and when he felt like taking a nip, down to the cellar he would go. One day shortly after he got the money from my mother, Zi Cesca, while visiting at our house, remarked to mother that she was sure Zi Toro had wine to drink. She said she did not know where he hid it, or indeed where he got the money to buy it.

We didn't have a real baseball or bat when we played baseball. The baseball was made from some railroad bearing waste fiber we tied with string. A carefully selected stick was used as a bat. The tree in front of our house, next to the street, was our only base. If boys wanted to play baseball they were called "bums" by their parents. Pat Parrillo said his father thought that he and his brothers would never amount to anything. When he went outside to play baseball, Pat would throw his ball or glove out the window first, and then sneak out of the house when his father was not looking.

When Pat turned 18, he told his Dad that he and Mary Mollicca were going to get married. His father said he would never allow the marriage. The Italians and others in town were perplexed. Please note here that Mr. Mollicca was a kind husband and father, and the Mollicas were considered one of the premier Italian families in town. However, Giuseppe Parrillo had few friends. It was well known by everyone in town that he beat his wife. It was said that each time she told him she was pregnant, he would punch her in the face; and when she fell to the floor, he would kick her in the stomach. Poor Mrs. Parrillo had a large abdomen. It seemed to me it was half her weight. When she sat down her whole tummy rested on her lap. Perhaps it was because she was pregnant so often. It was very sad that she was so terribly abused, and terrible for their children who witnessed the beatings throughout their young lives.

The Catholic Church requires a Baptismal certificate before anyone can be married. Pat was born in Italy. Of course his father told him he did not have it. Furthermore, he would not write to Italy to get one. Pat and Mary came to our house and asked Dad if he could help them get the certificate. Dad asked them both if they were sure that they wanted to be married. They both unequivocally answered "yes." He advised them to set the wedding date in eight weeks and he would take care of getting the certificate.

Dad wrote to St. Peter's Church, in Moiano, for Pat's Baptismal certificate and it arrived seven weeks later. The following week Pat and Mary had their wedding at St. John's Catholic Church. Mary's mother and father, my parents, and a few others were in attendance. For many years Pat and Mary lived with Mary's parents. They had one child, a boy, and they remain happily married. They are alive and well today. Both are over 80 years of age.

Several weeks after the wedding Giuseppe Parrillo belligerently said to Dad that he would like to know how his son managed to get that Baptismal certificate. Dad just shrugged his shoulders and said nothing.

Chapter

23   Move again, and again

The Erie Railroad completed the consolidation of the back shops in Hornell by 1935. The 90 year-old Susquehanna shops, which in the early years built steam engines, and later primarily repaired them, ceased to exist. Little note was made in town except the remaining few jobs that had survived the depression, were now eliminated. The roundhouse kept a boilermaker with one helper to do light repairs on the steam pushers. These two jobs were eliminated about 1947, when the diesel engines came into use.

In 1938, with no future prospect for work around Susquehanna, Dad decided to take his brother's advice, and announced we would move to Schenectady. My mother objected; she asked him if he had not gotten enough of his brother six years ago. In 1932 he had gotten completely fed up with his brother, and he seemed happy that his brother had moved to Schenectady.

Mother said, "After all that, you still want to go to Schenectady when you know very well he cares very little for you. Furthermore, why should we move to Schenectady? The work your brother writes about is only seasonal farm work and it pays very little."

To Dad it was work and he would be paid for it. Mother argued that, in Susquehanna, we still had our home, garden, and farm animals. Nevertheless, Dad sold our home to Paul McGuane, gave our cow to Zi Toro, and our household belongings were packed when the moving truck arrived.

In Schenectady, the first thing I noticed about our cousins was that Angelo was now called Chuck. Frank had a nickname, everyone called him "Speed," but Jack was still Jack. We now were in a big city and things were not any better.

During the summer of 1938, my parents, Marie, Anna, Zi Pasquale, Zi Rosa, Chuck, Frank and almost every other adult and older child who lived on Manhattan Street, went to the farms each day to pick beans. Mother prepared one meal each day, late in the evening when they returned from picking beans. I was left home with Lena because picking beans in the hot sun was no place for a frail 11 year-old boy, or a 7 year-old girl. An old neighbor kept an eye on us. We had not eaten breakfast, or lunch, so by the middle of the afternoon we were very hungry. It was because we were so hungry that Lena and I were introduced to the potato.

At the foot of our street (Manhattan Street), near the railroad tracks, there was an old oil drum and someone always had a fire in it. Many of the other kids put potatoes in the drum to cook. They got the potatoes in the cellar of our apartment, so Lena and I did the same. Over the summer Lena and I ate many potatoes, some quite raw and others burned. This is the only time in our childhood, or life for that matter, that we experienced hunger.

That fall I attended the fifth grade in Yates Elementary School. I had no problem with the teacher, in fact I enjoyed school, and one day it got better. Our teacher, I do not remember her name, asked the class to bring a newspaper article of national importance to school for the next days geography lesson. I went down to the cellar of our apartment and examined old newspapers stored there. I found one recent article about Secretary of State Cordell Hull's visit to Mexico. His goal for making the trip was to improve relations between the United States and Mexico. The next morning in class each student got up and read his article. When my turn came I read my article, but as I finished, the whole class burst out laughing. While I was accustomed to teachers not being nice to me, such an outburst from my peers made me feel quite lonely.

After all the students had read their articles, the teacher said that the best article had been mine. What a switch; this was the first time in my school years that I had received a compliment of any kind from a teacher.

In December of that year, destiny stepped in to guide our family. Apparently a neighbor on Manhattan Street reported us to the Schenectady Relief Department. The person or persons were certainly not acting out of loving concern. We had not applied for assistance because we were living on the proceeds from the sale of our home. Nevertheless, we were prime prospects to become future relief applicants. To prevent this, the department eliminated the out-of-state families who had moved there and were not employed.

Zi Pasquale, who had been supporting his family partly from bean picking in the summer and supplements from the $4,000.00 in proceeds he received from his house that burned down in Susquehanna, was concerned about the action being taken by the relief department. He went to the General Electric Works factory, and to his surprise, they hired him.

In late December, two men came to our door and ordered Dad to pack everything. They said our family must leave Schenectady and New York State in early January; the relief department would pay all moving expenses. They picked us up in early January 1939, in two automobiles and drove us to the Albany, Delaware and Hudson Railroad (D&H) passenger station. In Albany, they bought our tickets to Susquehanna, via the D&H to Binghamton and then the Erie from Binghamton to Susquehanna. At the Susquehanna station they offered to buy a meal for us and pay one nights lodging. Mother told them it would not be necessary because we had friends in Susquehanna.

I am sure this was a humiliating experience for my parents. As always, Dad did not say much, but mother made her feelings about the Schenectady move well known. From Susquehanna station, mother and us children went up to Zi Cesca's house. A day or two later, we rented a house on West Main Street.

Instead of accompanying us to Zi Cesca's house, Dad went directly to the roundhouse to see if work might be available. Fortunately, the roundhouse foreman received a message that very morning. It was to notify the next in line in seniority (Joseph Mango), to report for work as a boilermaker helper the next afternoon at the Hornell, New York roundhouse.

The foremen gave Dad a copy of the message and told him to go to the telegraph office and get a temporary pass. As he sat and listened to the click-clack of the telegraph, Dad waited patiently for the telegrapher to get the approval of the temporary pass from the superintendent's office in Hornell. He gave Dad a half-sheet of paper with these words on it: "To the Conductor of train number 7 January 10, 1939. This is a temporary pass, grant bearer Joseph Mango free pass from Susquehanna to Hornell, Tuesday January 10, 1939. Signed P. M. Donnellan, Superintendent."

Dad came to Zi Cesca's house about an hour after we got there. I could not remember seeing him so happy. He told us that he was called to work in the Hornell roundhouse and would start on the second shift the next day. Zi Cesca, who had great concern for our family during the depression, prepared a delicious spaghetti dinner. Zi Toro went down the cellar and, of course came up with a bottle of wine. It was one of the happiest meals we kids could ever remember. That night Dad, mother, Zi Cesca, and Zi Toro, stayed up late talking.

Excited about his good fortune, Dad slept very little that night. He was up at 4:00, got his dilapidated suitcase he had packed the night before, and headed to the station. He proudly boarded Number 7, which arrived on time at 5:07 a.m. When the conductor hollered "all aboard," the echo of the coach doors being slammed shut brought back many memories; how familiar this was to him. His memory went to the times he and mother took Giovannina to the Robert Packer Hospital in Sayre. By now mother was busy taking off Giovannina's coat and galoshes. He turned the seat in front so they had two seats facing each other. He had her lie across the empty seat to sleep. Mother adjusted her coat over Giovannina to keep her warm, and most often she slept all the way to Waverly.

As the train stopped at the coal pockets the conductor took the message from him authorizing his ride, dad didn't look straight at the conductor for he had tears in his eyes. He felt like a man once more, he had a job and could support his family. He hardly noticed anything as the train stopped in Binghamton for 21 minutes, and the short stops in Endicott, and Owego. When the conductor hollered, "Waverly, Waverly this way out," Dad gently shook Giovannina to wake her. As she sat up he put her galoshes on, mother struggled to get her heavy coat on and buttoned. Then she put her little knitted gloves on. Dressed with a new scarf around her neck, dad picked up his sick little angel and carried her off the train holding her close to keep her protected from the cold.

They quickly walked up one block from the Waverly station to get to the bus. That bus driver did not wait long after number 7 arrived. It took 25 minutes of stop-and-go riding to get to the Robert Packer Hospital in Sayre. Giovannina slept in Dad's arms all the way. After they got off the bus it was a cold, one block walk from the bus stop to the hospital entrance. As they walked in the hospital, the nurse recognized them right away. She came over to a smiling Giovannina, picked her up and carried her to a cold hospital room for the transfusion. She remarked that Genevieve looked very healthy and that she liked her new scarf.

Giovannina began to cry, knowing she would be poked with needles again. After a long wait the doctor came in. Dad smiled, he liked this doctor because he was always talkative and congenial. Not this time, however. Doctor looked at dad, with much agitation in his voice he said, "Joseph, I told you last time that your daughter is cured, why do you continue bringing her here."

When the door to the coach was opened, the noise of the coach wheels on the rails startled him out of his dream even before the conductor hollered "Elmira, Elmira, this way out." All the problems and worries that had been a greater part of his life during the 1930s seemed to melt away. As he wiped more tears, he felt great fondness for both his little girls who were taken from him. In his dream, Giovannina was happy and looked very healthy, an inner calm overwhelmed him. He had not felt this good since he had gotten his first job in America many years before.

He pulled his watch out of his watch pocket, a watch he had paid $60 for in 1913. It was 7:31 a.m., and number 7 was five minutes late arriving in Elmira. As the train left Elmira, dad realized that he was very hungry. He ate the two sandwiches Zi Cesca had prepared for him to take to work that afternoon. Even though he had never been in Hornell, he was sure that the station would be near a grocery store where he could buy bread and sandwich meat for that afternoon and evening.

He checked the timetable when they stopped in Corning and Addison; the train was losing time. It was a long time after leaving Addison when he saw sidings and extra tracks, then he knew the train was close to Hornell. He saw the roundhouse when the train passed it. Number 7 arrived at the Hornell station at 9:18, 21 minutes late. He got his little suitcase off the overhead rack and stepped off the train. He walked into the station waiting room, and from a window on the opposite side he could see a building across the street with a sign that read "Argentieri's Grocery Store."

He quickly went over to the store and bought a loaf of DiNardo's Italian bread for 10¢ and a pound of salami for 28¢. Still hungry, he went back to the station waiting room, tore the end off the bread and made himself another sandwich. It felt good to completely satisfy his hunger, and it felt good he had a job again. Soon he would have enough money to take care of all his family needs.

Edward Hungerford, in his book *Men of Erie*, stated that in 1938, the Erie Railroad was in the deep throes of bankruptcy. It had received a government reconstruction finance loan. The first priority late that year was to get some of the systems' steam engines back in working order. The rich Chesapeake and Ohio Railroad, which had held some 35% of Erie stocks from when Van Sweringens' owned it, sold it at a loss; a move that helped the Erie and secured a neat tax deduction for themselves. By 1941, a new and invigorated Erie emerged to face the next nine years as probably the best in its history.

Mother was disgusted with Dad because the Schenectady move had nearly depleted all the money received from the sale of our home. She declared that we would remain in Susquehanna, and not follow Dad wherever he wanted to go. Lena and I did not want to go to the Washington Street School, nor did Anna want to attend Susquehanna's High School. We felt we did not belong there anymore. Mother should not have unpacked our furniture, but instead should have forwarded it directly to Hornell.

Nevertheless, I was back in the Washington Street School for five more months, and nothing had changed. I can say there was no hair pulling by the teachers. Coyle was now the fifth and sixth grade teacher, and Lanning was the school principal. Marie, who had stayed in Schenectady for six months to graduate high school, returned in June. Never in the best of health, she looked fat, bloated, and pale. She stayed with poor relatives in Schenectady. Their meals consisted primarily of a cheap grade of macaroni with oil dressing. Mother blamed Dad for Marie's poor health.

The first thing Marie accomplished when she returned to Susquehanna, was to convince Mother the family should be together and that we should move to Hornell right away. I didn't get out of Washington Street School without another problem. When June came along, teacher Coyle, with Lanning's approval, decided they could not give me a passing grade. They said I had attended their school less than five months. The fact that I had attended a much better school, with a much better teacher, for the first four months of the school year, did not matter to them. They knew we were moving away from Susquehanna. Coyle and Lanning told me they were being very kind; they decided to give me a conditional report. A conditional report meant that I could be returned to the fifth grade by my sixth grade teacher. Be damned sure, if our family had remained in Susquehanna, teacher Coyle and principal Lanning would have had me repeat the fifth grade.

I should have been concerned by that conditional report, but I was not. Maybe it was because in my first four months in the fifth grade I experienced an excellent teacher and a much better school. I must have known that things had to be better once I got away from the Washington Street School teachers. I did well in my next school and the sixth grade. Furthermore, I worked three hours before going to school each morning.

Thank God, when I was 12 our family left Susquehanna, and I left the confines of Washington Street School.

I returned to Susquehanna in 1947 and found a boy I had started the first grade with was just graduating, whereas I graduated two years before him, in 1945. In my research I was told that in Susquehanna's High School, several of the teachers there were not any better. However, my sisters Marie, Lena, and others, admired the fairness of Dr. J. T. Yurkewitzh, the school principal. Dr. Yurkewitzh was a bright light that lit up the darkness that defined the Susquehanna public school system in the early part of 20th century.

Susquehanna was just another town in the northern Appalachian Mountains. It existed only because of the Erie Railroad. Other Appalachian Mountain towns existed because of coal being mined nearby, which Susquehanna did not have. The people in those mountain towns worked very hard. The conditions of their work, in many cases, caused their early deaths. In Susquehanna they worked equally hard. Many developed emphysema, and would suffer with this malady, which would later cause their deaths.

In 1883, if Ferdinando had not had his wallet stolen, the original individuals from Moiano would have not have gone to Susquehanna. Chances are the original group would have been directed to go somewhere else. Most likely it would have been no worse and probably much better than Susquehanna.

I feel adversity made me a better person. I highly recommend a sprinkling of this to be included in each life. Overcoming adversity when one is young builds character. This is the way I remember Susquehanna, not quite a lifetime ago, during The Great Depression.

612 Prospect Street as it looked in 1932, after a bathroom was added to the east front bedroom.

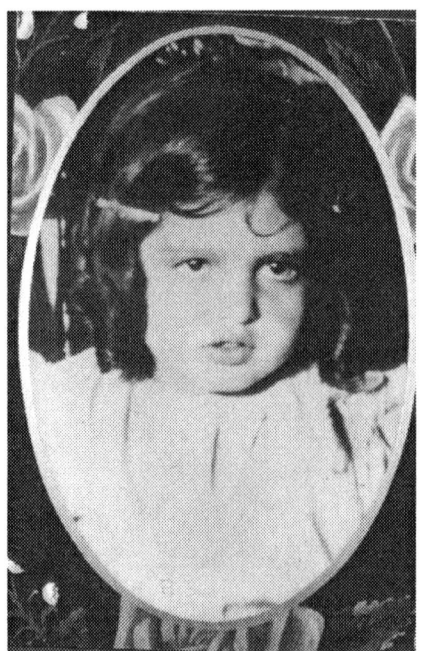

The second Giovannina, 1932.

The Giuseppe Mango Family Left to right front John, Lena, and Maddalena; back Giuseppe, Marie, and Anna 1936.

Passenger train of the period; The Erie Limited in the late 1930s.

Zi Toro & Zi Cesca in the late 1930s.

The Pasquale Mango family left to right Chuck, Zi Rosa Jack, Zi Pasquale & Frank 1937.

The author in his new shoes, pants, shirt, and most of all, his newly purchased second-hand bicycle, 1940.

Salvatore Grillo 1942 my best friend and fellow worker

Marie and Staff Sgt. Frank Mango our cousin on his visit 1945

Giuseppe Mango family seated front left to right Maddalena, Lena, Giuseppe; back Anna, John & Marie 1945

Chapter

24   *Hornell and Prosperity*

On Sunday, June 25, 1939, our household furniture was packed and sent on its way, bound for Hornell. We boarded The Limited westbound, Erie Train No. 1 at 1:43 p.m., to join Dad in Hornell. As a young child I experienced motion sickness every time I rode on a train or automobile. Most of my time was spent going from my seat to the lavatory.

As we looked out the train window, we wondered how fast the train was going because we saw the telephone poles go by very quickly. The wires that sagged between each pole had a rhythm of their own. After the train left Binghamton, the conductor called out strange towns names that I had never heard before. Endicott, Owego, Waverly, Elmira, Corning, Addison. Just before arriving at each station the conductor opened our coach door and shouted the station names. "O we go, Wav ver ly, L mira, and Add dis son."

I remember seeing many adjacent tracks filled with boxcars, other tracks had steam engines lined up as if they were ready to go to a parade. I could tell the equipment had been there a long time; grass and weeds were growing under and around that stored equipment.

Finally, the conductor opened our coach door and shouted, "Hornell, Hornell, this way out." As we got off the train, I could hear the hissing of air and steam. A mail and a baggage car were being switched off the front, and a coach taken off the center of the train. The switch engine was arranging the coach and a mail car, which made up the section of the train going to Buffalo.

The Buffalo train, scheduled to leave after the mainline train left for Chicago, would arrive in Buffalo at 7:35 that evening. No. 1 left 10 minutes after it arrived. Its route to Chicago, was by way of Meadville, Pennsylvania, Youngstown, Akron, and Marion, Ohio, and Hammond, Indiana, to arrive in Chicago 7:55 the next morning.

Hornell's topography is just the opposite from Susquehanna's. Most of the town and the ensuing area are flat. In 1939 it was a city of 15,000, quite large compared to Susquehanna, and it had existed before the coming of the Erie. The Erie, over its history, contributed greatly to Hornell's prosperity.

The first white settler, Benjamin Crosby, came to the present site in 1790. The first name given to the area was Upper Canisteo. The town was named Hornellsville for a George Hornell, an Indian trader who settled in the Hornell area in 1792.

The New York Lake Erie and Western R. R. reached Hornell in 1848. At the same time, car shops were under construction. By 1852 a branch line was completed to Buffalo. Hornellsville, thereafter, became an important center on the growing Erie system.

Shortly after the turn of the century, Hornellsville's growing population, now numbering into the thousands of citizens, dropped the "ville" and Hornellsville became Hornell. Erie's decision, in 1928, to centralize most of its steam engine repair shops in Hornell, added to the depression woes of Susquehanna and other shop towns. At the same time The Great Depression was not as severe as it might have been for those living in Hornell.

In 1935, heavy June rains caused the Canisteo River to overflow its banks. The following morning, Sunday, June 7, most of Hornell was under six-feet of water. The picturesque bridge across the Canisteo River at River Street had no overhead structure but had concrete arches beneath to support it. The arches complicated matters during the flood. Trees and large debris coming down stream could not pass through the arches; the bridge quickly became a dam, which contributed greatly to the diversion of the water across the city.

Dad was waiting for us when we got off the train. He happily led us up the platform and around the south end of the station to the sidewalk. We walked up River Street, by the Esso gas station, past Elizabeth Street to Front Street, then right down Front Street. Dad proudly introduced us to some of our new neighbors who were outside on that warm June afternoon. "Questa e la mia moglie e famiglia." (This is my wife and family). The last house on the south side of the street was number 110, our home during the World War Two years.

After five years with virtually no money to raise his family, coupled with being alone for five months in Hornell, Dad was proud and pleased that his family was together again. When we moved in the house at 110, there was a wood stove in the kitchen. My job each afternoon was to saw pieces of wood to stove size, from the pile of wood Dad had in our back yard. I soon found that the box saw I was using was just the right size. Bending over, resting the center of my chest on the wooden end of the saw, was comfortable and did not hurt. I then picked up a piece of wood, held each end, ran it up and down on the saw blades to cut it. I did this for several months when I noticed that the center of my chest had developed a small cavity.

A short period later, Dad installed a gas stove in the kitchen and a gas heater in the living room. Thereafter we had no need for firewood, or a woodcutter. The box saw still survives; it hangs in our garage, and has never been used again to cut firewood or any other kind of wood.

Later on, when my family began to notice my chest, Marie took me to Dr. Hertz, who examined me and proclaimed in spite of it, I would live a normal life. For many years it bothered me very much, I thought that I was not as normal as other boys.

Hornell was an exceptional town. Our neighborhood (including Front Street, River Street, and Elizabeth Street) was primarily Italian. I do not remember encountering any prejudice during those years anywhere in town. For me, even to this day, I could not think of a better place to have spent my teenage years.

Our family was now facing good times. Marie, flipping the pages of a Montgomery Ward catalog, figured the family could afford the refrigerator pictured on sale for $98, or payable at $9 a month. Indeed, she purchased the refrigerator and made the payments over the next 12 months. Three weeks later a Montgomery Ward truck delivered our first refrigerator. What a wonder, ice cubes were always available for the cold drinks. Milk was always cold in summer or any time of the year.

Shortly after arriving in Hornell, Mother found a best friend, Concetta who lived on South Street, just a few steps from our house. Mother and Concetta remained friends for the rest of their lives. Her husband worked for the Erie, and they had two daughters, Mary, and an adopted daughter Eleanore, who was younger.

With money to buy the necessities, Dad and Mother were enjoying life again. Dad was working full time, Marie was working, I would soon be working; prosperity attended the Giuseppe Mango family. Marie immediately got a job as a housemaid, and a week later she went to work in a dress mill. Several weeks after that, she accompanied mother to our new family physician, Dr. Hertz, a German Jew who had escaped Nazi Germany with his family in 1938. He persuaded Marie to come to work for him, and he paid her more than she could have earned at piece work in the dress mill. She continued to work for Dr. Hertz until she was married in January 1946.

By now adults knew that the Armistice signed in 1918, had not ended all wars. Hitler and Germany were leading the world on a collision course, and that collision was not far away. For us kids the world was as peaceful as it had been all our young years.

The first item on my agenda was to enroll in Bryant Elementary School. In late August, mother sent me there with the report card clearly stating, "passed on condition." The school secretary read my report card, raised her eyebrows, and then directed me to the sixth grade classroom. I walked into the empty classroom and introduced myself to the teacher, Miss Kemp, who was seated at her desk. As she scanned my report card, she reached into a desk drawer and took out a test. She told me to sit down, gave me a pencil, and told me to complete it. I was not happy, I had not even started school and here I was taking a test. I wanted to be back home; the other kids were playing handball. I completed the test as quickly as I could, and handed it to Miss Kemp. She told me to remain in my seat until she returned.

Four or five minutes later she walked back to the classroom. She smiled widely as she excitedly proclaimed, "Johnny, do you realize that you have an IQ of 138?" I really didn't know what she was talking about, IQ, to me, were just two letters of the alphabet. From her attitude, and by the way she said "Johnny, I will see you when school starts in two weeks," I correctly surmised that I was officially in the sixth grade.

That year the sixth grade was exceptional. I was the teacher's pet. Miss Kemp put me in charge of the bulletin board. I played a good part in the Christmas play. All the problems I had with teachers, thank heaven, were forever left in Susquehanna.

Lena told me in the middle of the following year that Miss Kemp had gotten married and apparently, either left Hornell, or teaching, or both. I do not know to this day if she continued teaching school somewhere else. I am forever very thankful that she was the sixth grade teacher at Bryant Elementary School those many years ago. If I was a child again, and I had to repeat the adversity of the Washington Street school, and if I were assured that I would have Miss Kemp as my sixth grade teacher, I would gladly repeat the fourth grade. I have nothing but good thoughts for all the teachers I had in Hornell. If God allowed me to go back and see just one of them, I would, of course, seek out Miss Kemp. If I could find her today, I would express my deepest gratitude and thanks that she was my teacher in the sixth grade, almost a lifetime ago. God bless her.

For our family, and all in America, World War Two ended The Great Depression. One day all radio broadcasters were saying, "Germany invades Poland," "England and France advised Germany they would declare war if Hitler did not immediately withdraw their forces from Poland." Thereafter, radio news and headlines included, "England and France declared war on Germany." World War Two had started.

I kept a scrapbook of newspaper headlines (Poland falls in 28 days) and articles that told of other battles. We learned a new German word "Blitzkrieg." A little later in 1940, the Germans took France, Belgium, Netherlands, Denmark, and Norway. It seemed for a time they would take the island of England.

Russia's Stalin, an anti-Christ second only to Hitler, entered the campaign against Poland, a few days before Poland surrendered. For his trouble, Stalin got the eastern half of that country. He, I am sure, was planning to get everything when the greater war ended between Germany, Italy, and England. Had Germany taken England and Ireland, World War Two may have lasted 3 to 5 years longer. Hitler greatly shortened the War by one of his many blunders; he overestimated the strength of his German Army when he invaded Russia.

Hornell had four movie theaters; The Steuben that showed all first-run pictures, The Majestic, The Hornell, and The Strand. The Strand had all the favorite movies for teenaged boys. For 11¢, I spent many Saturday and or Sunday afternoons watching Gene Autry, Hopalong Cassidy, and other western hero movies, and occasionally my favorites, "The Dead End Kids." And for a lot of laughs a movie featuring "Abbott And Costello." It was good to be able to go to the movies any week I wanted. I no longer had to collect Spaulding bread coupons.

One Saturday in September, I went to the movies and saw my favorite western star, Gene Autry, in a movie named "South of the

Border." The main song in the film sung by Gene Autry was "South of the Border Down Mexico Way," which became, and still is, a favorite song of mine. I remember humming the song on my way home.

Just before school started, I was told that the Italian baker on Elizabeth Street, Carmen DiNardo, was looking for help. I decided to go see him and I quickly had a job. The next morning I awoke with a feeling of great excitement. I quickly dressed, ran downstairs, out the side door and around the block to the bakery. The most important thing I felt then was that I had a job. During each weekday I worked from 5:00 a.m. until 8:15 a.m. On Saturdays I worked from 5 to noon. I woke up, without an alarm clock, promptly at 4:50 each morning, skipped breakfast, dressed, ran around the block to the bakery to arrive for work at 5:00

Most mornings when I arrived at the bakery, Carmen was singing "Cieleto Lindo," while kneading the raised dough. To this day I can close my eyes and still hear him singing that song. Soon he would form each loaf by hand. The first thing I had to do was to carry in more wood for the oven fire that was already going strong. And be sure there would be enough for the next morning. Carmen put each loaf in the oven with a long wooden pole that had a wooden plate on the end. The first bread out of the oven was the American style loaves; I ran each through a slicer. The sliced loaves were set on wax paper wrappers. I then wrapped each, and applied heat to each end, sealing them. When the Italian bread came out of the oven, I put each loaf in a long paper bag. I then put all the bread on small racks and carefully loaded the racks in the back of the bread truck.

Once in a while Carmen would accidentally damage a loaf of bread while he was placing it in, or retrieving it from the oven. When this happened we ate the remains, this was as close as I ever came to eating breakfast. Even now I do not care for bread. However, freshly baked Italian bread has always been the exception.

By the time the racks were all loaded in the truck, I was on my way to school; classes started at 8:30, and Carmen was on his way delivering the DiNardo Bakery bread to private homes and the city grocery stores. On Saturdays, while Carmen sat in the bread truck, I delivered the bread to each store and home. Carmen told me to place the remaining day old loaves in front, and the new fresh loaves in back on the store shelves. In the winter, Carmen occasionally delivered stale bread to some of the homes. On Saturdays, when I was making the delivery, if there was a complaint I was supposed to tell the customer that the bread had froze. I was not at all happy to do this. When asked I would say, "Mr. DiNardo said the bread had froze."

My stated weekly salary was all the stale bread our family wanted, plus 50¢. When Carmen paid me on Saturday, he would reach in his pocket, and appear to give me all of the change he had. All of the change he had never exceeded 30¢. The bakery was next door to Carmen's in-laws. I think their names were Caruso; Mr. Caruso, who seemed to me to be 80 years old, smoked cigarettes. He asked neighborhood kids to buy tobacco for him. He rolled his cigarettes, and he smoked them in his cellar.

One day, one of the boys came to me and asked if I would buy the Bull Durham tobacco for the old man. Bull Durham tobacco came in a little cloth sack with a small package of cigarette paper attached. The boy said he was not going to run errands anymore because the old man never once gave him even a penny for his trouble. I felt like the cat who just swallowed the canary, I told him I would. I thought, that dumb kid doesn't know the old man could help him after he died if he did favors for him now. I believed, even at that young age, that when you die, you discarded your body. The individual's spirit or eternal entity lives on, and could help us poor living souls. I am sure that people have spirits or eternal entities, or if you wish, guardian angels, helping them all their lives. Also, be sure if the individual they are helping does not live up to God's teaching, the spirit can also mete out punishment to them.

I have always tried to be careful and not incur any life debts. By debts I mean in the conduct of one's life, and relations with other people. If you take something that does not belong to you and you are not caught, most people in our society think that they got away with the theft. I would rather be caught and be punished immediately. Whether you pay man's penalty for doing wrong you surely must pay God's. God's punishment can be much worse than man's.

How many times in this life have I heard an individual proclaim, "Everything bad happens to me", I believe that with just a little honest investigation into the person's actions, a reason would quickly be found.

Each time Mr. Caruso asked me I would run both ways, to and from, Joe Camadaga's grocery store to buy and then deliver the Bull Durham to him. I did this for several weeks, until he died.

Dad and mother noticed that I had a constant cough throughout the winter months. For that reason they decided it was best that I did not work at the bakery anymore. Mother notified Carmen of this one Saturday morning after he had brought me home for the day. I cried because I lost the job, and tears came to Carmen eyes when he realized he no longer had me as his employee.

In May 1940, Dad decided that we would visit our friends, Filippo Palma and his family in Hoboken. We all boarded No. 2, and eight hours later Zi Filippo met us at the Jersey City station and took us to his tenement in Hoboken. We ate well at the Palma residence. In those days whenever friends came to visit, Italian families bought and prepared the best foods for their visitors. The morning after we arrived, we went back to the Jersey City station where we boarded the Chamber Street Ferry. I remember the cool breezes as we crossed the Hudson River. We then went to Mulberry Street; it probably did not look very different than it had when Dad's brothers took him there in 1913. Mulberry Street was special for Dad. It reminded him of his arrival in America as a 17 year-old, and as a newlywed a few years later when he and mother visited the street in 1920.

Chapter
25 *Carefree Teenager*

One morning I woke up to a lot of noise. Behind our house, near the river, big construction machines were moving dirt. The widening of the channel for the Canisteo River and the construction of the new River Street Bridge began. This large construction equipment uncovered much scrap metal. For quite some time I made good money collecting that scrap metal and selling it.

The construction of the new River Street Bridge and the flood control project cost seven million dollars. It was started early in 1940 and it lasted for more than a year. It eliminated flooding in the Hornell area for the balance of the 20th century.

I remember when the crane, with a large steel ball, appeared one morning and they began to demolish the beautiful bridge. The replacement steel bridge had much overhead structure. River Street, at the Canisteo River would never look the same again.

They built a temporary wooden walkway to cross the river. Over the next year we children got a good view of the demolition of the old bridge and construction of the new bridge. I enjoyed our family's new prosperity. I had some money to spend. The biggest treat was to go to Elmhurst Dairy Store on Erie Avenue and buy a milkshake. The milkshakes were thick with ice cream and cost 15¢.

Most of the neighborhood boys had their own two wheel bicycles. I asked Mother if the family could afford to buy me a bike. One day, in the spring of 1940, Marie, mother, and I, went uptown to the J. C. Penney department store. They bought me new pants, a matching shirt, and new shoes. On our way back home we stopped at the bike shop on Broadway, next to the fire station, to price bicycles. A brand-new all chrome bicycle cost $60. It was a beautiful piece of machinery, but the cost was way out of our family's price range. The shop had one in our price range; a secondhand Roadmaster for $15. Mother counted out two five dollar bills and five ones and the bicycle was mine.

Nothing but good things, were happening to me since our move to Hornell. I was in heaven. New shoes, new shirt, new pants, and most of all, the bicycle I wanted. Total cost for all, approximately $18. It was probably the most money spent on any child in the Giuseppe Mango family, to that date.

I took good care of that bicycle, repaired flats, kept the bearing greased, and the brake cleaned periodically. I eventually gave the bike a new coat of paint. The bike lasted until just before I graduated high school.

One afternoon every week, after public school, the Catholic children went to Saint Ann's School, to prepare for Confirmation. The priest and nuns instructed us, and we practiced, practiced, practiced, for what seemed to me to be weeks and weeks. The choice of a sponsor was very important for Dad, and all Italians, because that person would become "Compare" (Godfather). Dad decided to ask a friend's son from Schenectady, Francis Palmo, to be my Godfather.

Finally, Confirmation weekend came. Francis Palmo arrived Friday night with his father. It was a festive weekend, and then finally it was Confirmation Sunday. Because we had practiced so much, everything went well at church. That afternoon Mother prepared a big three-course pasta dinner. The best part for me was that my new Compare gave me a gold-plated Westfield wristwatch. I took good care of the watch, and it lasted me until after I graduated high school. I do not remember ever seeing my sponsor again. The ways of the Italians in Italy were changing for those in America.

Boys in our neighborhood joined the Boy Scouts. I needed other experiences so I went along and also joined. How proud we all were to be Scouts and members of Troop 70. We attended every meeting held on Thursday evenings, downstairs in a business building next to the Majestic Theater on Broadway. The weekend scout camp in May was an exciting time. Mother gave me 25¢ to spend, but rationing it over the three days was challenging. I managed to buy an ice cream cone Friday night, a coke and an ice cream cone on Saturday, and an ice cream cone on Sunday before we left for home. Camp Gordon, the big two-week scout camp, was held each August. The cost was too much for me even to mention at home. I do not think any other member of our troop went to Camp Gordon.

As time passed, our scoutmaster had to work overtime on the Erie, and he began to miss meetings. A short while later he ceased to be a scoutmaster. For a couple of months we did our best to conduct the meetings and remain a scout troop, even without a scoutmaster. One Saturday, our troop, without a scoutmaster, joined in a large scrap paper drive. We worked from 8:00 a.m. until after dark collecting old newspapers. We came in second, even though the other scout troops we were competing against were much larger, and better organized than ours.

The Fourth of July was a big day for all the scouts. We marched in the parade. On that second Fourth of July parade, our troop, such as it was, took the same place we were in the year before. As we were waiting for the parade to start a scoutmaster came by and advised us that we were in the wrong position. He led us back, way back to the last scout troop at the rear end of the parade. On our way back there, I got a closer look at the other scouts. Most boys had full uniforms with several merit badges pinned on their scout shirts. We had merit badges too, but only a few of us had scout shirts. Those without scout shirts had the insignia and Troop 70 sewn on one of their better shirts.

I felt we were just a rag-tag bunch of boys. It was embarrassing to see how well organized the other troops were, and it was embarrassing to be shunted to the rear of the parade. Nevertheless, we received applause from the few people still watching the parade when we went by. When the parade was over, all the scouts were supposed to meet in the park, in front of the high school, to hear speeches. Free refreshments would be served. I decided I was in the wrong place and headed for home. The rest of the troop went home also. This ended Troop 70 and my Boy Scout career.

Making model airplanes from balsa wood kits, bought at the hobby store on Main Street, was fun. The most popular kits sold were of the Japanese Zero, the German Messerschmidt, the English Spitfire, and later the American P-39s, P-40s, and the F4U Corsair. When the plane skeletons were completed, special paper was glued on the body, wings, and tail parts. After the glue had dried, water was sprayed on the paper. As the paper dried it shrunk, eliminating all the wrinkles. Then the wings and tail were glued together, completing the model.

I was not very careful when making models, they did not look as good as the same models my friends assembled. I soon tired of my poor work. I took the models upstairs, lit the plane's tail, and out the window it would go, ending up in a fiery heap 8-feet below on the ground.

One day, I bought a large maroon stamp book at the hobby store. I became a stamp collector. I looked at every old envelope I could find, in case it could contribute another stamp for my stamp book. The hobby store sold little cellophane packages that contained 15 to 20 assorted stamps for 25¢, which I bought occasionally. The packages contained stamps from far away countries such as Sierra Leone, Belgian Congo, British, Dutch, and French Guiana, Ceylon, and a host of other countries.

One day, I put one 25¢ cellophane package inside another. The old gentleman who owned the store could not see too well. I paid 25¢ for two packages. Because stealing bothered me, I didn't do it again.

I soon tired of collecting stamps and I put my stamp book away, which contained 400 or more stamps. I kept that stamp book for many years. When I was moving items from home to our apartment, after Pia and I married in 1956, I noticed the stamp book was gone. I never did find out what happened to it.

For a while, my best friend was Buddy Whalen. We played handball, horseshoes, and did many other things together. In the spring, the Canisteo River usually had enough water in it to float a raft. The boys across the river made themselves an excellent raft by nailing one by two slats across four old railroad ties.

We were very jealous watching them maneuvering their raft up and down the river, like Tom Sawyer and Huckleberry Finn. One cold day we found the raft on our side of the river. We laughed, as we got on it. With pieces of scrap metal, we began breaking it apart. We laughed even harder when one tie, then the second, and third, broke away. Buddy was smart. Instead of trying to balance himself on the last tie, he jumped in the river and got wet to his waist. Not me, I tried to balance myself and fell backwards in the water and got soaked. I sat with my wet clothes on for some time, before I decided to go home and put up with Mother's wrath.

Shortly after the incident, Buddy moved across town and we did not see each other anymore. Another boy my age (I don't remember his name) became my best friend. We did everything together. His parents had moved to Hornell from Jersey City. One day he told me they were moving back to Jersey City. Thereafter, for the most part, I was less inclined to have too many close friends.

After school was out, in the early summer of 1941, Salvatore Grillo and I heard that they were hiring on the Muck Lands, located on the other side of the town of Arkport, six miles from Hornell. The Muck Lands is decomposed wood; it is black in color, and is very fertile. One morning we hitchhiked there, and the first farmhouse we stopped at hired us. We worked ten hours a day, six days a week, and we were paid 15¢ an hour. This totaled $9 a week. The end of that first week, late Saturday afternoon, because Carmen DiNardo never paid me the agreed weekly salary, I was amazed that the farmer paid us $9. Each morning I was up at 5:45, went around the corner to Elizabeth Street to meet Salvatore. We walked down River Street to Loder Street, then across Broadway to Seneca Street to North Hornell. As we walked we were oblivious to everything else around us; our discussions centered on subjects interesting to young teenaged boys.

In North Hornell we started to hitchhike. Rarely did we arrive late at the farm for our 7:00 starting time. Hitchhiking 6 miles up each morning and back each evening, we were away from home from sunrise to sunset.

The farm raised celery and lettuce. Most of what we did all summer was on our hands and knees. With our hands we loosened the dirt around each lettuce and celery plant, at the same time weed roots were exposed, which killed them. The farm had about 10 fields planted, a total of 60 acres. We probably did all 10 fields three times before the plants matured.

Salvatore and I competed against each other. We used to get on parallel rows and see who finished the row first. Sometimes we started on opposite corners of the field to see who got to the middle first. It is not too hard to surmise that the farmer loved us.

Later that summer, during harvest time, trucks from Philadelphia came to take the produce to market. The smaller celery stalks and lettuce heads were left on the field. The farmer allowed us to fill large net bags with the leftover lettuce and celery.

We got on the road to hitchhike home, carrying the large sacks stuffed with the lettuce and or celery. Sometimes the bags we carried were as large as we were. Many of our neighbors on Front and Elizabeth Streets had all the lettuce and celery they could eat during harvest time that summer, those many years ago.

I remember evenings when we were left off downtown. We then walked up Loder Street with the big sacks of lettuce or celery. A Chinese man who ran a laundry often stood in front of his store. Several times he remarked, "You have lettuce today boys?" I now know that he would have been very happy to receive a free head of lettuce, or stalk of celery. Unfortunately, I don't remember either Salvatore or myself giving him one.

Chapter
26 U.S. enters the war

Late that fall, on Sunday afternoon, December 7, 1941, at about 4:30, I walked out of The Strand theater after seeing a Gene Autry western, and a paperboy was across the street from the theater loudly proclaiming, "extra, extra read all about it, Japs attacked Pearl Harbor!" Before television, when something important happened, the newspapers quickly printed an extra edition.

I rushed home. Dad was listening to the radio. News reports were about the details of the Japanese attack. All that evening, we listened to the radio reports, telling of the names of the ships sunk, and those badly damaged. The following day the United States declared war on Japan. Hitler and Mussolini declared war on the United States; America was at war.

Before the attack by the Japanese, Americans did not want to fight someone else's war. The Japanese changed all that. I believe that the British, who had the best military intelligence, were advising our government of the Japanese fleet movement. Due to this information, it was not hard to surmise that Hawaii and Pearl Harbor was the probable target. Roosevelt took no action, he felt a Japanese attack would stir the American people to support a war; and it did. He left our fleet anchored at Pearl Harbor, to take the losses of ships and lives; he however made sure that America's two aircraft carriers were not at Pearl Harbor that Sunday morning.

Right after Pearl Harbor, the government sent people of Japanese descent, on the west coast, to detention centers. The still untold story is that many naturalized Italians and resident aliens, some who were in America more than 20 years, were also sent to detention centers.

In March of 1941, Danish, German, and Italian ships, in American ports were seized. Twenty-eight Italian ships were seized including the *Conte Bianca Mano* cruise ship. It was stopped at the Panama Canal and boarded. All 480 passengers including women, children, and crewmembers were interned. The *Conte Bianca Mano* was the ship Mother and my two surviving sisters returned home from Italy in 1925.

Employees of the Italian 1939 World's Fair pavilion in New York, and many immigrants who had not yet gotten their citizenship papers, were sent to detention centers. On the east coast, Ellis Island became a prison. Some, who had the happy experience of successfully making it through the facility years before, had the ignominious experience of being sent back there as prisoners.

There was much more of this detention activity on the west coast. Soon it didn't make a difference if an Italian was naturalized or not. Some Italians interviewed by the television program "Histories Mysteries," on the "History Channel," said this detention of Italians was lead by west coast Army General Dewitt. He made it his job to make life for Italians miserable. In Oakland, California, one side of a street was designated as a military zone and the other side wasn't. However, on the military zone side, an Italian grocer had to close his store, and lost his livelihood. All Italian fishing boats on the west coast were confiscated, and Italians were not allowed to fish. Fisherman's Wharf was declared a military zone. The parents of Joe DiMaggio, a baseball star, had a restaurant there. They were forced to close it and were not allowed to set foot on Fisherman's Wharf.

Vast tracts of some cities in the west were designated military zones from which Italian resident aliens were evacuated. It is estimated the total number of Italians detained was 10,000. Within 24 hours after the Japanese attack on Pearl Harbor, the FBI compiled a list of resident alien Italians, and Germans. The FBI, armed with telex search warrants, searched alien Italian residents homes; radios, cameras, and flashlights were confiscated. Many Italians were taken away at night, their assets frozen. Many were taken in and there were judicial hearings. None of them were allowed to have an attorney present. During this period, Italians were sent to detention camps in San Antonio, Texas and McAllister, Oklahoma. By far the biggest Italian detention camp was an old converted army fort in Missoula, Montana, surrounded by chain-link fences and guard towers.

All Ellis Island detainees were later sent to Missoula. All activities of this sort were conducted with the approval of President Roosevelt. He was not concerned about the Italians on the west coast. The detention of the Japanese was all over the radio and print media. All government action against Italians was not known by the large concentration of Italians in the east and mid-west.

Then, in the summer of 1942, it was said that mayor Jack Rossi of San Francisco was seen giving a Nazi salute. He was taken into FBI headquarters and questioned. Newspapers ran the story and it reverberated all the way to the east coast. New York mayor Fiorello LaGuardia quickly got Roosevelt's attention. Roosevelt was concerned only because midterm elections were coming up in the fall. He knew that the loss of the Italian vote in the northeast and mid-west could spell disaster for his party. He instructed Attorney General Francis Biddle to make the announcement on Columbus Day 1942, that the government had watched Italians for nine months, and they were considered loyal. Harassment of Italians was stopped. Roosevelt wasn't watching Italians or anyone else, because he was too busy playing Commander in Chief in Washington, and spending time in Warm Springs, Georgia, with his concubine.

Since the fact of the Italian detention camps were still not known by Italian voters in the east, Roosevelt decided that those already in detention camps would be left there. They finally were released in the fall of 1943, after Italy surrendered. Most unfortunate for the Japanese in

America, was that they did not have a large concentration of their brethren in the northeast and mid-west, for which Roosevelt might be concerned should they vote against his democratic party. In the end both the Italians and Japanese in America cannot complain very loudly.

The poor Jewish souls in Europe were most unfortunate. Their Jewish brothers in the United States were more concerned about losing Roosevelt's friendship, than trying to save their brethren from the Nazi death camps. Roosevelt knew that the Jews in America were not going to vote for anyone else but him, no matter how he handled the German death camps problem.

Roosevelt had full knowledge of the death camps and where they were located by late 1942. In June of 1943, a contingent of Americas prominent Jewish Rabbis went to Washington to meet with Roosevelt, to urge him to bomb the crematoriums, and the rail lines leading to them. Roosevelt sent word that he was busy with appointments that afternoon and could not see them. We now know that he had no appointments the afternoon in question. Some historians now try to put the blame for his inaction in Washington to various departments, such as State and War.

Early in 1944, a bipartisan committee of congress decided they would convene a hearing, to determine why nothing was being done to save those poor Jewish souls. Fearing the scandal that would ensue, Roosevelt quickly issued an executive order that set up the "War Refugee Board." Its purpose was to attempt to save European Jews. The hearings were then cancelled. This belated effort is credited for saving close to 200,000 Romanian Jews.

Hundreds of thousands of American and British bombers dropped millions of tons of bombs over Germany during the war. Much of the time the bombers flew over the death camps, on the way to bomb other targets. Sadly the death camps were intact and still working to full capacity within hours of being overrun by American, British, and Russian armies.

In the weeks and months to come, the Philippines, Burma, many Pacific islands, and even two of the Aleutians Islands, fell to the Japanese. It was necessary to listen to the Lowell Thomas broadcast each evening, to keep up with the increasing pace of the war. Network news correspondents, who gave on-the-spot reports from London, and other war areas, made the news even more interesting.

Mussolini sent his army to invade Ethiopia, Albania, and Greece, with foot soldiers armed with guns, few trucks, and no tanks. The only difference between Mussolini's army and the American Civil War armies of General Lee, Sherman, and Grant, is that the Italian army had trucks that on some terrain could go faster than horse drawn wagons, used by the aforementioned generals.

As late as 1940, the whole of the Italian army had two tanks. They were used only in maneuvers, and were transported by truck to each location. Mussolini sent two hundred thousand Italian soldiers to the desert of North Africa, with few trucks and no tanks.

In early 1940, the British had virtually lost to Field Marshal Rommel's tanks, German, and Italian soldiers. After Rommel captured Alexandria in Egypt, because the German army was embroiled in Russia, Hitler lost interest in the African campaign. He ignored Rommel's request for more tanks and other mechanized equipment.

Meanwhile, the British received reinforcement for their Eighth Army with many new American tanks. By 1942, British General Montgomery started a large offensive against Rommel's tanks and Italian soldiers. Rommel, seeing defeat close at hand, notified the Fuhrer of his predicament.

In William L. Shirer's book, "T*he Rise and Fall of the Third Reich[1]*," he tells of the war in North Africa in 1942 as follows: *"Bad news reached the Fuehrer from another front. Field Marshal Rommel's Afrika Korps was in serious difficulty.*

"At long last the British army in Egypt had received strong reinforcements. When it launched a major offensive late that October Rommel was in Austria on sick leave. By the time he got back to his army, the battle was already lost. The British had too many guns, tanks and planes, and though Rommel made desperate efforts to shift his battered divisions to stem the various attacks, he realized that his situation was hopeless. He had begun to withdraw when a message came from the supreme warlord: (Hitler) "There can be no other consideration save that of holding fast, of not retreating one step, of throwing every gun and every man into the battle. You can show your troops no other way than that which leads to victory or death."

"This idiotic order meant, if obeyed, the Italo-German armies were condemned to annihilation. After a struggle with his conscience, Rommel reluctantly gave the order to halt the withdrawal. But two days later, at the risk of being court-martialed, he decided to save what was left of his forces and retreat. Only the remnants of the armored and motorized units could be extricated. The foot soldiers, mostly Italian, were left behind to surrender. Within 15 days Rommel had fallen back 700 miles to beyond Benghazi."

The few trucks and tanks that were left by Rommel with the surrendering German and Italian foot soldiers were not in running condition. Rommel, by his action, saved thousands of German foot soldiers, and some 200,000 Italian soldiers. Left with no armored units, and virtually no food or water, the German and Italian soldiers had two choices. One was to fight the British tanks with rifles and die under their guns. The other was to surrender. The odds were stacked against them. They made the wise choice and surrendered.

---

[1] Edition copyright 1987 Brompton Books

During that period there was much said in news broadcasts about the surrender of Italian soldiers. The movie newsreels showed pictures of some German soldiers and many thousands of Italian soldiers surrendering to a handful of British tanks. The news footage over the years has left a lasting impression that the Italians were afraid to fight.

I wasn't pro Nazi, however these were Italians soldiers. My cousins and many hundreds of thousands of Italian immigrants sons were fighting for America. I did not believe that they would run from a fight, and we know they didn't.

In Hornell, and every other town in America, young men joined or were drafted into the armed forces. Before almost every Erie passenger train left town, mothers and fathers bid tearful farewells to their young sons. Many of those boys would not return.

Soon the towns and cities across the country became devoid of young men. Only young boys, like myself, were left. When we chose sides for a ball game, the older guys, whom everyone wanted on their team, suddenly were not there anymore. The most dreaded occurrence for families was a Western Union telegram from the War Department notifying the parents of the death of a son.

In Schenectady, our cousin, Chuck, wanted to join the Marines right after Pearl Harbor, but his Dad would not give his consent. However, four months later, his Dad changed his mind and approved of his enlistment. Boot camp in Perris Island, South Carolina, quickly made Chuck, and all other recruits, into men. Chuck distinguished himself as a Marine Master Sergeant in the South Pacific.

On the island of Pellalu, Chuck went to get his issue of battle gear for the planned landing of the 3rd Marine division, at Leyte Gulf in the Philippines. The sergeant issuing the gear said, "I am sorry Sergeant Mango, I issued you battle gear this morning." Chuck, perplexed, replied, "Sergeant I was not here this morning." "But you were," was his reply. Chuck asked, "Please check your records."

The sergeant took a minute or so to scan his list, and apologized, he had issued gear to a Sergeant Joseph Mango who was in a different battalion on the other side of Pellalu. The next morning there was a small Mango reunion when Chuck located Joseph Mango, Zi Bernardino's son, our cousin.

Joseph visited Chuck on the following day, he waved goodbye as Chuck boarded the troop transport plane. Joseph forlornly watched Chuck's plane take off. He stood there as two other planes left, before he went back to his unit on the other side of Pellalu. He knew that come tomorrow, it would be his turn to go.

Later, Chuck and Joseph were in the second wave of the invasion of the Japanese island of Iwo Jima. The Marines fought their way up Mt. Surabachi. As Chuck's company was reaching the top, several Marines ahead of his company were replacing the American flag with a larger flag. This became the most famous photograph of World War Two.

In the fall of 1942, cousin Frank enlisted in the Army. The Army sent him to Officers Training School. After a couple of months Frank worried that he would spend the entire war in school and not see any action. He quit the school and volunteered for active duty. Soon after D-Day, Frank, a Master Sergeant in the elite 104th infantry division, (Timberwolves), crossed the English Channel with some of General George Patton's 3rd Army. Four months later, it was George Patton's 3rd Army that broke the Germans noose around remnants of the 104th and General McAuliff's 101st airborne division in Bastogne.

At home, the Big Bands were good entertainment. Each evening, one or two of the big bands were featured on the radio, The Dorsey Brothers, Glenn Miller, or Harry James, just to name a few. The radio broadcast originated from such far away places as The Glen Isle Casino, The Hollywood Palladium, Frank Dailey Meadow Brook, and many other dance halls around the country.

Saturday night at 9:00 we listened to "Your Hit Parade," one of the most popular radio programs. It featured the top ten songs in the nation each week. During the summer, when the hit parade was on, most homes had doors and windows open and radios tuned in to the broadcast. You could hear the broadcast anywhere on Front Street. The songs I liked the most were "Maria Elena," "I'll Get By," "I'll Walk Alone," and many others.

We kids on Front and Elizabeth Streets didn't have any parks to play in. We learned to improvise; we played touch football and baseball on the street. We used the concrete seam on the center of the street to play handball. Tody Lucecco and I were the champions at handball. Tody was one of the neighborhood boys I missed the most when the Army drafted him.

Soon we noticed that on the end of Front Street, next to the railroad tracks, the Erie had removed all the junk. They left a dirt area big enough for a baseball field. All us kids spent a week or two clearing our way for a baseball field. We laid rocks in the ground for the bases, had foul lines, and soon, we had a pretty good field.

One day we scheduled a game with the boys from River Street, whom we did not like. I was not much of a hitter or fielder. Nevertheless, I played center field in that game. I got a hit and scored a run. We won the game. The score was something like 12 to 8. A couple of the boys from our team went to the *Evening Tribune* to tell the sports editor about our victory.

The following day, in the sports page, there was a small headline that proclaimed, "The Front Street All Stars drown the River Street Rats." The article went on to give the details of our victory.

One morning on my way to school, as I looked over at our field, the railroad was dumping coal on it. The coal mounds would be 10 to 15 feet high. That coal remained on our field for the rest of the war.

One fall day, when I was in the seventh grade, four or five of us boys were walking down Main Street, on our way home from school. Just up Main Street from the school was a fruit store. The owner had a bushel of apples outside, in front of his display window. The apples were the largest I had ever seen. One of our group suggested we run by the store and each grab an apple. We all thought it was a good idea. So we got into a line and as we ran past the store, we each grabbed an apple.

Five of those huge apples almost filled the bushel basket. The owner started to run after us. Very soon I heard the owner running close behind me. I was running as fast as I could. I do not know where the other guys went, but Johnny Carbone was running abreast of me. I knew that at any minute the owner would grab my shoulder.

At the first corner, Seneca Street where we crossed, the light was green. On the other side of the street, because the light was red, Johnny Carbone turned left and headed east on Seneca Street toward the post office. Because it was my way home, I turned right, across Main Street against the red light and headed toward Liggets Drug Store.

Apparently the storeowner, not wanting to come after me against a red light, headed after Johnny. As I crossed the street I heard cars screeching to a halt; luckily for me I didn't get hit.

I quickly walked up Main Street, then right on Broadway to Loder Street and home. I had no desire to eat that apple. I left it on a windowsill of an abandoned store on Loder Street. I was relieved and felt very fortunate that the owner had decided to pursue Johnny Carbone instead of me. Thereafter, on my way to school and home from the 7th grade, I crossed the street before the fruit store and walked on the opposite side. That frightening experience literally ended my career as a thief.

I decided I was with the wrong company when, shortly after that incident, I met one of the boys in front of the dime store on Main Street. He had a bag full of 5¢ packs of Beechnut gum. His partner would go into the store, hang around the candy counter 30 or 40 seconds. Then he would come outside and hand his buddy another hand-full of candies and gum packets. A few minutes later he went back inside to repeat his little trick. I didn't want to have anything to do with their thievery; I completely detached myself from this gang.

I did not use my bicycle during bad weather conditions. One late fall day while I was walking to the 8th grade class at the high school, I happened to look down at my feet as I walked. I didn't realize it before, but I noticed that I was throwing my left foot inward. I had visions of how Zi Giovanni (Crooked leg John) walked. He threw one foot in, and was slightly bowlegged. I was not bowlegged, however I walked quite a bit like he did.

I did not want to be known as "crooked leg John." For many, many weeks thereafter, as I walked to school, I consciously guided my left foot to point straight ahead as I took each step. At the same time, I threw my shoulders back and held my head erect. My posture was not a problem, I was only making sure that it would not become one. I was oblivious to anything happening around me as I walked to school, because I was concentrating on my left foot.

For some time, after I was completely satisfied I had corrected my left foot; I continued to watch that I was not throwing it in any longer. I finally won, both my feet pointed straight ahead as I walked.

The following summer, Salvatore, and I went back to work on the farm. The farmer was so happy with our work the previous summer, he asked us to stay at his house all summer. He provided room and board at no charge. We still were paid $9 per week so it seemed we had gotten a raise. The biggest benefit for me, from that summer's stay on the farm, was breakfast. The farmer's wife prepared a big breakfast each morning; fried eggs, bacon, or ham, toast and milk. That summer was probably the healthiest period of my childhood.

At home we always had plenty to eat; mother was an excellent cook. She cooked southern Italian dishes for lunch and dinner, but she didn't make breakfast. In Italy, the family left for *coppa monte* very early in the morning; breakfast was not prepared.

That second summer on the farm we had much fun. Occasionally we worked on a Sunday. One Sunday, in early July, when there were four adults present, the farmer decided to cultivate the rows of young celery plants using the tractor. Salvatore was shorter than I. He could not reach the brake and clutch pedal. I was taller and could just reach them. I became the sole designated driver. The tractor was an Oliver 70, the back wheels stood higher than I was tall.

The tractor pulled cultivators, which had to be guided by the adults between the rows of young celery plants. The farmer showed me the position of the different gears on the gearshift and to depress the clutch when shifting gears, and to depress the brake pedal and clutch to stop. He said put it in low. I did so and slowly let up on the clutch. I was amazed how easy it was to drive a tractor. It was fun and I was being paid for it. Well, sort of being paid, considering that the first day I drove a tractor was on a Sunday.

On that particular Sunday, a Front Street neighbor decided to visit my mother and Dad. While there, he suggested they take a ride in his automobile to visit me. This was a treat for mother and Dad because we did not own an automobile, and they had not seen me since the middle of June. Furthermore, they had never been to the farm where I worked. At the end of one of the celery rows I turned the tractor to start up a new row, I was then facing the farmhouse. I could see our neighbor and my parents walking toward the tractor. Mother and Dad had big smiles on their faces; their son was driving a tractor. I was happy to see mother and Dad and I was proud that they saw me driving a tractor.

I have always loved corn and I bragged all that summer that I could eat a dozen ears of corn if I wanted to. Salvatore did not think much of corn, however he bragged he could eat a gallon of ice cream if he wanted to. One day later in the summer, a truck from Philadelphia came to pick up a load of lettuce. That evening, when Salvatore and I returned from the fields, there was a large plate with a dozen of the largest ears of white corn I had ever seen at my place on the table. Where Salvatore usually sat there was a gallon of ice cream. The farmer, his wife, the truck driver, and a couple of neighbors watched while we attempted to eat our words.

I got half way through ear of corn number six and could not go on. Salvatore was only half way down into the gallon of ice cream, and he could not continue. Everyone had an entertaining evening. Thereafter, neither Salvatore nor I bragged much about how much ice cream or corn we could eat. That summer our farm work ended. That farm experience remains a pleasant boyhood memory.

Salvatore and I spent all day together the first summer on the farm. The second summer we were together all the time, from the middle of June to early September. I am now amazed that over those two summers we never once had anything like a disagreement. In 1993, I felt I needed some of Salvatore's memories of that pleasant experience. I was finally able to contact his brother, Jimmy, who lived in Mesquite, TX. I sadly learned that Salvatore had died in March of 1986.

At home, I was the designated mailer. Dad wrote letters to his brother in Schenectady, and later in the war when Italy surrendered, he wrote to his brothers in Italy. Dad insisted that letters be mailed at the railroad station. There were two mailboxes. One was west of the waiting room that read "West," I never had a letter for that box. The other box was east of the waiting room marked "East". Dad's letters always needed to go east, and that is where I deposited his letters. Passenger trains RPO (railroad post office) car clerks picked up the mail. Once in a while, I got there when No. 2 in the morning, or No. 8 in the afternoon, both eastbound trains, was in the station. I would walk to the RPO car, and hand it to the man near the door sorting mail.

The clerks in the RPO cars picked up and dropped off bags of mail at many stations where the train didn't stop. At the larger stations many bags of mail were dropped off and picked up by the clerks in these rolling post office cars. Passenger train RPO cars were important in those days, if one wanted to speed mail to its destination.

In the fall of 1942, I had heard the bowling alley behind the Majestic Theater downtown was short of pin boys. One evening I went to apply and got a job. Most of the week, there were not many bowlers. Two or three of us pin boys had to wait for the few bowlers who came in. On Saturday night business was brisk and we worked steadily.

Things went well for me until the men's league started on Thursday evenings. The manager was lucky if enough pin boys showed up to work, so he didn't have to set pins. That meant that a pin boy had to work two alleys; this became a problem for me.

The pin boy had to balance himself on a back ledge above the alley pit. When the ball came through he had to jump in the pit, pick up the heavy ball, and put it on the return. Then he had to place each pin in the overhead rack, which was at eye level, leaving the rack slots of the pins that had not fallen empty. He had to quickly jump over a three-foot divider into the second alley pit, return that ball and pick up the pins and place them in the overhead rack. Then jump into the first pit, return the ball, pick up the remaining pins, place them in the overhead rack. The pins rested at an angle in the rack. Then he had to grab the handle of the rack and lower it, the pins were in an upright position when the rack was at its lowest point. This released the pins on the alley floor. He had to lower the rack gently, or after it was released a pin might start rocking, causing it to fall. If the men got a lot of strikes this was harder for the pin boy, because he had to work even faster.

As the evening wore on I got tired and slowed down. The men playing on my two alleys were always the last to finish. At the end of the evening those playing in the other alleys would slide a 50¢ coin down the alley for the pin boy. As one could guess, I never got that bonus. I went home completely exhausted on Thursday nights. The only reason the manager of the alley did not fire me was that I was setting pins instead of him. Realizing how bad I was, on the fourth or fifth Thursday after men's leagues started, I quit.

The following April 17 of 1943, I was 16 years old. I heard that they were looking for help at the Erie freight house located next to the passenger station. I talked to the supervisor there and he hired me to work all night on Friday, and Saturday, with other high school boys.

We hauled bulk freight between freight cars, with the two wheel hand trucks. This work was extremely hard for a frail high school boy. After I worked there about three weekends the supervisor called me in and told me they did not need me any more. They needed more help; I could not understand why I was fired. However, at the time I was 5 feet 10 inches tall and weighed 128 pounds. Trying to balance those heavy loads on the hand trucks and at the same time having to maneuver the trucks between freight cars on metal ramps for bridges was not easy. Working as a freight handler was no place for me.

Along with all the adversity at work, I caused myself more trouble at school. Ever since we moved to Hornell, every teacher challenged me in every grade. I had worked much of the time, and I balanced my work time with my school studies and did quite well. All the teachers I had were excellent, and I got along with them very well.

Well, that is except for the ninth grade math teacher, I do not remember her name. In a half-size room, on the third floor of the high school, there were twelve boys in her math class. We all were doing very well until one day Carl Peterson, who lived out of town on a farm, brought in BBs taken from a shotgun shell. Carl apparently was bored with class. When the teacher looked the other way, he threw the BBs against the blackboard. As they hit they made a lot of noise. The teacher turned and asked, "Who did that?" Of course, no one said anything.

"If you do not tell me who did that, everyone will stay after class," she said. Unfortunately, it was the last period in the afternoon so we were her prisoners. She made us just sit for an hour doing nothing before she excused us.

I am not blaming Carl for our problems, the blame was shared by 11 of the 12 boys in that class, myself included. Anyway, the next day Carl brought in many more BBs and gave some to everyone. When the right time came Carl threw his at the blackboard, and as the teacher turned to look at his side of the class, I threw mine. When she turned to look at my side, someone on the other side threw their BBs.

Thereafter, she completely lost control of the class, and never did gain full control for the rest of the year, or gain any of our respect. The more she punished us, the more we disrupted the class. Instead of keeping everyone after class, she picked on two or three students at a time.

I was one of the first kept after class. The first afternoon she kept two other boys and me until 4:30. The next afternoon she kept us again. I was watching the clock. I did not want to stay again until 4:30.

About 4:15 she walked to the other side of the class away from the door. I got up and walked out, but she ran after me. I was already down three flights of stairs, as I heard her shouting at me to get back. The other boys took the golden opportunity and walked out behind her and went down another stairwell.

The next morning the janitor came over to me and asked, "What the hell was the teacher shouting about last night?" From then on she locked the classroom door whenever she kept us after school. I quickly decided to behave, and after that, I did not have to stay after school.

Scholastically we were all doing very well in math. Once a week she gave us a test, we all competed for the highest score. My test scores were always 85, 88, maybe 89, never above that. When I say compete, it was for the second, third, and fourth place, because Johnny, one of the boys in the class, always got the highest mark.

I remember many insignificant items of my past 73 years, most of which you will not find herein. But try as I might, my mind will not tell me Johnny's last name. He was an Italian boy. He always had the highest test scores, which were usually 95% or better. Furthermore, Johnny had nothing to do with our classroom shenanigans.

Near the end of the school year, I don't remember exactly how it happened, the teacher turned and it appeared that Johnny had misbehaved, which wasn't so. I could see how it appeared to the teacher that he had misbehaved. I told her it wasn't Johnny, and even though several other boys told her that Johnny had done nothing, she made him stay after school. We all felt that it was grossly unfair that she kept him after class when he was innocent. Even if he had been guilty just one time, it would have been unfair.

A few days later, Johnny came to me and said, "I'm dropping last period math." I replied, "Johnny, don't be so stupid, three weeks are left, you have already passed the class." Johnny, nevertheless, dropped math. Just before school ended in June, a special movie was on at The Strand Theater. Saturday at 12:30, like many other boys, I was in line to buy a ticket when the box office opened. Johnny was just in front of me. We were joking and laughing and having much fun. Johnny suddenly had become a good friend.

The following Monday, Johnny wasn't at school. Later, during that summer when I was working full time on the Erie, I heard he had come down with polio. I didn't know where they had taken him or how to contact him. I was upset that such a good friend had fallen ill.

Several years later, in fact it was the early 1950s, when I was working in the Erie ticket office in Binghamton, New York, Johnny called me. He was in a rehabilitation home in Corning. A few weeks later, crippled and walking very slowly with two crutches, he took a train to Binghamton, visited with me a couple of hours and then took another train back to Corning. I can still see Johnny struggling with crutches as he slowly maneuvered himself through the waiting room door.

I didn't follow Johnny's visit with one of my own to see him in Corning. In my life, I am sorry for many of the things I did or didn't do. I am most sorry for not having kept in contact with Johnny. I don't know if Johnny is still alive or, for that matter, how to find him.

Chapter
27 *Growing up*

All the steam engines the Erie had, no matter how old, were in service. In fact, earlier in the war, the Erie purchased several freight diesel engines for service between Marion, Ohio, and Meadville, Pennsylvania. It was after the war before Hornell got a good look at the diesel engine.

I can still recall the back shops and how they looked during those war years. Twenty-seven steam engines were dismantled and rebuilt at a time. When an engine was completed, it was pulled out of the shops and another engine was rolled in to replace it.

About the time school was out in June, Dad proudly took me to the Erie shops and introduced me to Mr. Nemo, the union leader. He assured Dad that I would be hired. I quickly learned he knew what he was talking about. I was hired to sweep floors in the back shops, full-time, 6 days a week from 3:00 to 11:00 p.m.

That fall my last class ended at three in the afternoon, but I got permission to leave 15 minutes early. I rushed home, got the lunch mother had prepared, and then walked to the shops. I clocked in to work each day just before 3:00. I was paid 55¢ an hour, a small fortune for me. I cleared, after deductions, over $60 twice a month. I gave most of it to Mother.

Leading two lives, my school life and my full time railroad shop life, was a busy time for a high school student. There were about ten high school boys who worked in the shops. Our foreman was Mr. Sexton. I do not remember his first name. Because he was short, we called him "Shorty." Shorty worked six days a week; however, he did not work on Saturday nights. He had to work Sunday nights when we did not work.

Ten high school boys, working without a foreman on Saturday night, was not a good idea. All over the back shops there were cans of yellow paint. The yellow paint was used to paint the engine number on each part as the steam engine was disassembled. This was done so the engine could be reassembled with its original parts.

We noticed that occasionally the shoe heels of some adults were painted yellow. If someone could paint your heels, it indicated that you were sleeping on the job.

We thought this was a good idea, so on the following Saturday night, during a long lunch period, we decided to paint heels. If the employee was running a lathe we had to sneak behind him, and work very fast before he saw us. If the person whose heel you were painting realized what you were doing, you quickly disappeared into some other part of the large back shops.

In the area where all the disassembled engines were kept, a riveter might be up in a firebox with his feet hanging out, a perfect target for a high school boy with the intention to paint available heels.

After a couple of weeks, we decided that we were not organized enough; too many of us were being caught. I suggested that two of us should approach a likely prospect and ask the most serious question of the times. "Which engines were better, steam or diesel?" As I said before diesels were already in service on the west end of our line. The diesel repair shops were already established in Marion, Ohio, not in Hornell.

We high school kids did not know how serious our question was. The old steam men knew that their jobs would not be needed in the near future, when steam engines would be replaced by the diesel engine. In fact, all of the steam jobs were eliminated over the next five years.

The first victim we engaged in a discussion was attaching cables on engine parts. He got hot under the collar when we said, "we knew by good authority that diesels were not only better, they were far more powerful."

While the crane operator up above was watching, the best painter in the shop, Jimmy Grillo (Salvatore's brother), was painting the victims' shoe heels. Jimmy did an excellent job. No paint got on the shoes only the heels were yellow. Many times, after Jimmy was gone, and we didn't like how the discussion was going, we would call our victim a "sh-- heel" and walk away.

Because we were painting close to a dozen pairs of heels every Saturday evening, complaints about us were so numerous, that it got the attention of the shop superintendent. Our fun was ending anyway, by then most of the men had become aware of our strategy.

One afternoon we were all called up to the superintendent's office. The superintendent told us that if this didn't stop at once, he would fire all of us. There is no way he would have fired us, because they were already short of workers. At that time the Erie would have hired any, and every high school boy, if he just applied for work.

A few nights later, Shorty asked me if I thought I could learn to drive the hi-low truck. I replied, "I could," just stretching the point a little. I told him I had driven a farm tractor last summer when I worked on a farm.

The hi-lows were pallet trucks and were used to transfer wooden pallets full of engine parts from one part of the back shops to another. It was fun. As the driver, I stood on two pedals on the back platform. One pedal operated the brakes, and the other pedal was the clutch. Lifting one foot, the brake was applied, and lifting the other foot the clutch was disengaged. The gas lever and the gearshift were near the steering wheel. All that and my pay went up to 79¢ an hour. I learned very quickly how to drive a hi-low truck. It really wasn't much different from driving the farm tractor. From then on I was too busy to play games with the other high school boys, or ever consider painting heels again.

One night, when it was snowing, foreman Shorty said, "Johnny, don't take that short-cut tonight because you will get stuck in the snow." It wasn't really shorter; it was longer. However, with nothing to slow me down, I could go from one end of the back shops to the other at top speed. I thought to myself, "I'm driving, you aren't."

The first chance I got to take the short cut, out I went and quickly got stuck in the snow. A few minutes later, while I was trying to get the truck moving, Shorty came out and pushed me until I got back in the shops. He never said a word to me. After I graduated high school, Shorty, God bless him, came to see me but I wasn't home so he talked to my Mother. He asked her to talk me into coming back to work with him in the shops again.

It was the spring of my junior year in high school. Every day at 11:30 a.m., I went home for lunch. After eating my lunch, and before I was due back in class, I generally had 15 minutes to spare. With school time and working eight hours on the railroad, those 15 minutes were about the only spare time I had. Joe Camadaga's grocery and cigar shop on River Street was on my way to school. Joe had a wooden leg, or one leg was crippled, I don't know which or why. Anyway, Joe had two pinball machines in his store. Feeding nickels in Joe's pinball machine took up 15 minutes and caused me to lose 25¢ every day.

I was hooked on those machines. Five afternoons every week I stopped, exchanged a quarter for five nickels, fed every one of them into Joe's machines. Each day I did this, I felt guilty and it was embarrassing to spend that much money just to play the machines. Each day after lunch, I would say to myself, "I am not going to play those machines again." Try as I might, I couldn't go by Joe's store without stopping.

A couple of the boys who were playing the machines most lunch hours occasionally used a corset stay instead of nickels. Slip one end of the flat thin stay under the medal slide that took the nickel and bingo, a free game. Those boys played for free, right under Joe's nose.

I didn't realize it at the time but apparently Joe felt sorry for me. Each Friday he asked me to dust the store shelves and he paid me 25¢. Instead of losing 25¢, I earned 25¢. Joe didn't know that I was working 8 hours a day, six days a week on the railroad and being paid 79¢ an hour.

I felt I was not strong enough personally to quit the machines, so in desperation, I asked God to give me the strength to quit them. God granted my wish, but not in the way I would have chosen. One day, as I walked in Joe's store, a boy motioned me that he was leaving and he left the corset stay partly in the nickel slot of the machine I usually played.

The temptation was too great to pass up. I asked Joe for my usual five nickels for a quarter, made a noise like I put one nickel in the slot. I pushed the lever with the stay in and it was easy. Suddenly Joe said, "What are you doing?" and very quickly, bad leg or not, he was right behind me. There was nothing I could do I was caught red-handed.

He took the stay out of the machine, and said, "Thatsa whata you do, I giva you soma work so you cana earna soma money anda to thanka me, you steala froma me!" He told me to get out of his store and never come back. I couldn't figure out how the other boys who had been cheating him for many weeks didn't get caught. I couldn't get started in one free game and I got caught. It upset me to have done something so stupid. I was also embarrassed that everything Joe said was true.

Each afternoon, thereafter, I would sneak a look in Joe's store as I passed it. Many of the same guys were playing his machines. I don't know if they were playing for free or not. I didn't care anymore. I had lost all interest in pinball machines. The extra fifteen minutes I had, I now needed because I started my last year of high school.

During those war years there were many shortages; meat was rationed, gasoline was both scarce and rationed. Lines formed in front of any store when they had women's silk stockings or cigarettes for sale. Cigarettes were given to servicemen; the government encouraged them to smoke.

In 1988 the Surgeon General of the United States declared that cigarettes were addictive and harmful to your health. What a revelation! I knew that in the 1940s. I began to smoke at age 15 because most of my peers smoked. Several years later in my middle twenties, realizing that smoking was harmful to me, I fought a tremendous personal battle to finally quit smoking them.

One winter morning I awoke with a sore throat and fever. I was so sick that I stayed in bed. By the following morning my fever had reached 105. I became delirious and thought I could hear myself talking although I wasn't speaking.

That morning at work, Marie's employer Dr. Hertz showed her a sample of a new drug he had just received. She insisted that he go to our house and administer it to me right away. I was the first in our town to get a penicillin shot. Thirty minutes after the shot my fever dropped to 100. I felt almost well enough to go to school. During the war, penicillin was a miracle cure and it saved many of our wounded soldiers' lives.

In the later period in high school, when anyone asked me a question I didn't want to answer, I replied, "ask uncle Pete." I wasn't referring to any particular person. It was just my way of avoiding the question.

Italy surrendered before the end of the War. Dad received a letter from Zi Pietro. He wrote that the war had left them destitute. Dad, terribly upset for his brother's problems, sent him most of what he had saved along with the $300 mother was holding for me. "Uncle Pete fixed you good," my sister Anna said. Dad later repaid me $500.

The Erie had no woes during the war. It went through the best period of its railroad life. Bankruptcies, receiverships, and reorganizations seemed to be behind it. Freight traffic was so heavy that if one train had troubles and stopped, behind it another dozen trains were also delayed. Passenger trains were running full, and in many cases, a second and third section followed.

Our troops were primarily transported by rail and Erie got its share. On my way to, or coming home from high school, I passed the passenger station. Many days I could see a troop train pull in and local canteen girls were there to meet it. They handed the soldiers candies and cookies through the trains open windows. I could see that all the coaches and dining cars on these trains were not Erie's equipment. I learned names of other railroads, such as Illinois Central, Union Pacific, Santa Fe, Milwaukee, Soo Line, and others.

In early 1944, the roundhouse foreman in Susquehanna called Dad back to work there. He accepted, because he would lose all his accumulated seniority had he not returned.

I had worked six days a week all the previous summer. Then all winter I worked full time and went to school full time. Soon school would start and I would be back to that long daily schedule again. Dad worried that I worked too hard. One weekend in early August, when he came home from Susquehanna, he told me to take a week off and spend it in Susquehanna with him at Zi Cesca's house, where he was boarding.

On Sunday morning we headed for Susquehanna, the only place we could find a seat on Erie number 2 was in the smoker section on the end of one of the coaches. Before we left Hornell, the Buffalo/Jersey City train coaches were added to our train (Chicago/Jersey City). Many passengers were standing in the Buffalo section when it arrived in Hornell. After the train left Hornell those standing in the Buffalo section, came into the Chicago/Jersey City coaches looking for seats, but none were to be had; people stood in the aisles throughout the train.

In our smoker alone, at least a dozen men were standing, and most were paying passengers. About 15 minutes after the train left Hornell, a mother and her teenage daughter gave up by the time they reached our smoking section. Instead they selected a good place to stand.

Dad quickly got up and offered the mother and daughter our seats. I felt good because the teenage girl was looking at me with a loving smile. That is until Dad explained to her mother, that we were deadheads riding on free passes; railroad rules required us to give up our seats to paying passengers.

Like some of their fathers did during The Great Depression, some of Susquehanna's teenage boys spent much of the day standing around downtown. I spent most of that week downtown talking with them. I felt wonderful because I knew that next week I would be back in Hornell to my full time job. Standing around, doing nothing has always been alien to my psyche.

I was happy to return home, because, I had many mosquito-like bites all over my body. Dad later told me the bites were from bed bugs.

The following week, I became concerned that I would not graduate high school until 1946. I now realized the culmination of the incident when I was in the fourth grade when, I was unfairly held back by Miss Ryan. Thoughts of graduating sooner than 1946 began to occupy my mind. Later, in August, I went to the high school and got class schedules. It didn't take me long to figure out that if I dropped my homeroom periods, I would be able to take all the courses I needed to graduate in June 1945.

Just before school started I went to the principal's office and told him of my intentions. His reply was, "Such a thing has never been done before therefore I cannot approve your request." I left the principal's office depressed. I had no control of those past years when I was unjustly held back. I had some control now. Something must work. If things had been different I would be starting my last year of high school.

Several days later an idea came to mind. I wondered why I didn't think of it sooner. The following morning I again went to see Mr. Cook. He had a look on his face that said I told you no and I mean no! I said, "Mr. Cook, next April, I will be 18 and I will be drafted in the Army. I would like to graduate high school before I enter the Army." He sat for a minute or two, tapping his pencil on his desk, silently thinking. It seemed like an eternity to me. Suddenly he asked, "Do you have the schedule worked out?" As I began to describe my plans he interrupted with, "Go to it, son."

I had won and I had lost, I would graduate high school in 12 years. However, I traded a superior high school year with excellent teachers for an inferior grammar school year, with, at best, questionable teachers.

In January 1945, I resigned because I didn't want to continue as a hi-low driver on the railroad after graduation. I spent the last five months of high school just concentrating on my studies. The Erie was short of telegraph operators so, in January of 1945, they started an evening class to teach telegraphy, in which I enrolled. In June, three of us completed the class, William Rockwell, Francis DiVincenzo, and myself.

· All my life things seemed to be pre-planned for me. All I had to do was follow the plan and everything worked out fine. If I didn't follow the plan, whatever I tried would not work. If I insisted on a plan of action not apparently pre-ordained, I was stopped in my tracks. For instance, throughout high school, I didn't date any girls. I was very shy, besides I had no time. I had just turned 18 and I would be graduating in two months; it was time I should consider a girlfriend, indeed, a wife.

There was one girl in whom I was interested I will call her Peggy. She was attractive, shapely, intelligent, and quick-minded. I just idolized her. If she had asked, I would have done anything for her. I decided to ask Peggy to go to the movies with me. It didn't occur to me that I probably could have arranged to run into her at school. That Sunday I got on my bike and headed to Peggy's house. Peggy lived a long way from our house and walking there would take too long. I pedaled my bike up

Front Street, then down River Street and Loder Street, downtown under the subway, we called it that, it was only the railroad underpass.

Going down the subway my bike chain broke and was dragging on the ground. I stopped the bike at the bottom of the underpass and found it had just come apart. After a few minutes I found the chain link lock that had fallen on the street. I put the chain back together and started again for Peggy's home. I went less than five feet and the chain came apart again. It had come apart in another place. I quickly put it together. Less than 10-feet up the underpass, the chain broke.

I certainly wasn't going to push the bike all the way to Peggy's home and back. I walked the bike home, repaired the chain, and I still couldn't get it to work. The following week, I bought a new chain. Taking it for a test run around the block, halfway up Elizabeth Street the new chain broke. I was frustrated; I had always kept that bicycle in good repair without any problems. Now something seems to stop me from using it.

The following weekend I continued to try to make the new chain work. I checked the alignment of the front and back sprockets of the bike. They were aligned okay. The back wheel was tightly bolted to the frame, and it was aligned okay. The roller bearings in the sprocket and back wheel housing were okay. There was no play in the sprocket or the back wheel. Without the chain, I turned the sprocket quickly and I could see it was not warped. For the first time in almost five years during good weather, I had to walk to school.

One day the following week, as I was maneuvering my way through the crowded hallway to my next class, a student I hardly knew stopped me and asked, "Do you know Peggy?" I was surprised by his question and replied, "Yes I do." His answer was very short; it indicated she had very loose morals. I was upset by the words of a virtual stranger about the girl I adored. He wasn't even sure I knew her. I was upset for some time and wondered if she wasn't really the girl I thought I knew.

The plans for my marriage eventually came, however it was 10 years in the future. When I met my wife, Pia, she was everything I used to think Peggy was.

In April, I received greetings from the government to appear at a time and date in Buffalo, New York, for my Army physical. There were about 30 young men who boarded the morning Erie train for Buffalo. A bus met us at the Lehigh Valley/Erie station and we were taken to a building where we were told to remove all our clothes.

My sister Marie had told me that I might be rejected because of the depression in my chest. Furthermore, by now the war was winding down and the Army's need for new recruits had greatly diminished.

After I spent two hours moving from one line to another, the last doctor who looked at me asked if my health was affected. I honestly replied, "no." Anyway, he stamped my papers 4F; I was rejected for Army service. Another time in my life I failed, and again I was embarrassed. When we returned on the train, everyone but me speculated where they would be stationed after they were inducted in late June.

One evening in the middle of May, there was a knock on our front door. To everyone's surprise and delight, dressed in his Army uniform proudly displaying his sergeant's stripes and Timberwolf insignia was cousin Frank Mango. One of the first things he did after spending a few days home in Schenectady, was to take the train to Hornell to visit Zi Peppino, Zi Maddalena, and of course Marie, Anna, Lena and myself.

Frank stayed three days with us. We all listened intently when he told us of some of his Army experiences. I especially was interested when he told about being surrounded in Bastogne, during the battle of the Bulge, in December of 1944. He said that all the soldiers' morale went up when they heard that General McAuliff's reply to German General Mantoifel's surrender demand was, "NUTS."

I asked Frank many questions during his visit. One was, had he met any of the local people in the countries he fought in. I quickly realized how dumb the question was. Frank replied, "I met British, French, Belgians, and especially the Dutch." I replied "The Dutch!" Frank went on to say, "Yes! The Rotterdam Dutch, the Amsterdam Dutch and all the other damn Dutch," I laughed the rest of that evening.

Frank was shipped to the west coast and would have been sent to the Pacific, however, the war with Japan ended before he was scheduled to leave San Diego for the Pacific. Both he and Chuck were discharged in later 1945.

After a while, because I wasn't working any longer, I began to do things high school boys of this period did. After school I would stop at "Rawady's Two Door" where most of the kids stopped after school for coke and ice cream. I would order a coke, though I didn't much like coke. I liked strawberry sodas, but it cost 20 cents. My favorite was a banana split that cost 35 cents. Since I no longer was earning money, my experience with poverty didn't permit me to spend any more than the 5 cents on a coke. It was fun when I occasionally stopped at the pool hall and played pool with some of the boys.

One of the girls, I don't remember her name, was the star in the senior play to be performed the middle of May. She said they needed a stage manager and would I take the position. Of course, I said I would. At the last minute they asked me to do a bit part near the end of the play. They probably felt sorry for me because I had worked so hard to position the scenery during each brief intermission.

It didn't occur to me at the time, but it was the only high school student activity I had participated in. Alas, the brief period of being just a high school student quickly came to an end. Graduation night, June 25, was a proud day for me; I had graduated. I cannot know now how my high school life may have been different, had I not worked. I do not regret the path I had taken during those high school years.

My thoughts now centered on a job as railroad telegraph operator. I had completed the telegraph class and I was ready to start work right away. As much as I had enjoyed our days in Hornell, I later found it very easy to leave the town where I had spent all my carefree teenage years.

I was out of school and I was unemployed. For the first time in years I had no plans for the day. J. P. Hogan, the chief train dispatcher and our telegraph class instructor, said he would call me when a telegraph position opened. That wasn't good enough, so each weekday and Saturday morning at 8:00, I went to the station, walked upstairs, and stood outside his office until I could get his attention. I left when he said "No, not yet."

Finally, by later July, sick of seeing me, he offered me the position of Telegrapher/Freight Agent in Tioga Center, New York, which I accepted. On Thursday morning August 2, 1945 without eating breakfast, I proudly boarded The Erie Limited No. 2, at 11:00 for Owego. No passenger train stopped at Tioga Center.

J. P. Hogan told me to sit on the south side of the coach, and after the train left Waverly, about 14 minutes, I would see Tioga Center Station. Sure enough, we whizzed by the station that had a freight room and a former passenger waiting room. In between them was the freight office. I can still see this station in my mind's eye, even though it was 55 years ago. In 1989, during our visit back east, we stopped in Tioga Center. The station was still standing but abandoned, the doors and windows were missing. The station was left to the elements to eventually collapse.

Chapter
28 *World War Two ends*

The war with Germany ended in April, and that month President Roosevelt died. Hitler committed suicide in his bunker in Berlin. The Russians later identified his remains. Stalin survived the war. For the next forty years he and his Russian successors caused the United States and other western countries to spend much money to keep a strong military defense. Unfortunately, that money, if spent for peaceful purposes, would have greatly improved the world we live in, and World War Two may have actually been the war to end all wars.

Shortly after I began working in Tioga Center, President Truman decided that by using the atomic bomb the war with Japan would quickly end. In early August the first bomb was dropped on Hiroshima. A couple of days later another was dropped on Nagasaki. Japan quickly and unconditionally surrendered ending World War Two.

All of Dad's accumulated seniority in Susquehanna did not help a year later he was laid off for the last time. Mother and Dad returned to Hornell where he went to work as a car inspector. Anna was employed by the J.C. Penney store in Hornell. Lena graduated high school in Susquehanna, in 1947.

Marie's sweetheart, Staff Sergeant Salvatore Palma, came back from the Marines in the Pacific. They married in January of 1946, and rented an apartment near where Sal worked in Jersey City. Marie and Salvatore had two daughters and 5 grandchildren.

Later, Anna traveled to Europe where she met American Air Force Lieutenant Monte Piper, who was stationed there. They married, had three children, two girls and a boy, and ten grandchildren. Anna and Monte now live in Humble, Texas.

Lena went to college and became a teacher. During her first teaching job she fell in love with a fellow teacher, Robert Tarbaux. They married, also had three children, two girls and one boy, and four grandchildren. Robert died at age 65 in 1992; Lena now lives in Rialto, California.

And as for myself, I have been married for 44 years, have two sons and one daughter and all three of my children have two daughters each, giving my wife and I six beautiful granddaughters. We now live in Irvine, California.

America's prosperity continued after the war. Life as we knew it before World War Two had changed for the better. We assumed the world had also gotten better, but lasting peace would continue to elude us from 1945 to the end of the twentieth century.

I left Hornell, and would never live there again. During the years of World War Two, and at the age I was, I couldn't think of a better place where our family could have resided. I doubt that anyone living in Hornell during that period would disagree with me.

Hornell's population decreased after the war. With the coming of the diesel engine the work force in the shops were drastically reduced. By the 1980s Hornell ceased to be a railroad town.

Hornell is a much different town today. It is not that young, vibrant, growing community that it was in the 1930s and early 1940s. It takes its place among the little towns of America, resigned to no real future.

The Italian immigrants, who had come to America in the early part of the 20th century, were now in their 50s and 60s. The sons and daughters of these tough Italians had reached adulthood. During the war hundreds of thousands of them gave distinguished service to their country, and many never returned.

The respect for our parents, uncles, aunts and all the rest of that generation continues. I can remember the lectures from my parents, relatives, and other Italian immigrant friends, who told us kids to always stick together. "Eacha you stay together, anda be prouda che sei Italiano, anda be happy che yu are Americano, Capisci? Do yu understanda?" These words will forever be etched in my mind.

Most of the immigrants continued to maintain vegetable gardens until their deaths. In the middle of the summer they called attention at how well their tomato crop was. They proudly showed their grandchildren their gardens; offered them fresh tomatoes, carrots, radishes, and cucumbers, when they visited.

I am proud of that generation who immigrated to America; they were not welcomed and faced tremendous adversity. Their only goal was to provide a good life for their children. As they got older they beamed with pride to welcome American grandchildren, and a few lived to proudly welcome American great-grandchildren.

Dad, Zi Pasquale, or Zi Bernardino, never talked of any abuse received from their father. However, dad visited Moiano in 1952. Zi Pasquale made the same visit in 1953. When each returned, I asked them how each enjoyed the trip. My Dad's reply was, "No, se avessi potuto, sarei tornato a casa il giorno dopo" (If I could have, I would have come home the next day). Zi Pasquale's reply to the same question was, "No, avrei solo voluto vedere quella pietra in coppa monte dove ho pianto tutta la mia gioventù." (I just wanted to see that rock, *coppa monte*, were I shed all those tears as a child).

Of the three brothers who remained in America, Zi Bernardino was the first to die. At the age of 70, in April of 1963, he died four days short of his 71st birthday. Zi Pasquale out-lived every one of the Italians who immigrated to Susquehanna. He died in 1988, at age 93, surviving his wife Rose by two years. Dad passed away in December of 1966 at age 71 years and 5 months. Mother passed away in July of 1986, at age 88. Marie died at age 49 of breast cancer in November of 1969.

Dad was most happy when he worked, no matter how hard or dirty, or how many hours per day. Most importantly to him, he was supporting his family. He savored fried hot pepper sandwiches in the summer, or pasta prepared with oil and garlic topped off with several red cherry peppers mother had canned the summer before, or a dish of polenta. When we were children, at the dinner table, he waited until all of us said we wanted no more before he would then finish what little was left.

Mother watched over her family well during our childhood years. Because she was an excellent cook, we always ate better than most of our neighbors. Even today I cannot enjoy eating in an Italian restaurant; nobody prepares Italian food anywhere near as good as she did. She lived long enough to witness 11 grandchildren grow up and she proudly counted 8 great grandchildren before she died. I am very proud to have had parents such as these in this lifetime

America, the land of opportunity for Italians and other Europeans earlier in the last century, continues to be that land for the poor from Mexico, Central America, and many other countries. Many Americans today talk of the illegal immigrants entering the United States. They express the wish that these illegal immigrants be returned to their homeland. If I were in the immigrant's place, I would be doing as they do; that is to come to America legally or illegally to seek a better life.

During the great European immigration to America, many had to traverse foreign countries before they could board ships for America. Because of that, they needed passports to get to the port of exit. The Italians needed no papers to board ships at Genoa, Naples, or Palermo for America. Subsequently, my father, relatives, and many other Italians, were illegal immigrants. I am profoundly thankful that during the early years of the 20th century these illegal immigrants were allowed to stay, work, and establish their homes here in America.

End

Appendix
The Erie Railroad

Some geographical facts of the Erie R. R., not generally discussed by railroad historians, are important to understand the plight of the old Erie. Four eastern railroads had New York as their eastern terminal and Chicago as their western terminal. They were the Erie, New York Central (NYC), Pennsylvania (PRR), and Baltimore and Ohio (B&O). The Erie did not do as well as these other larger railroads of the northeast for one reason; the other railroads had substantially more population bases along their lines.

There were eleven large cities, with a population of 100,000 or more, that the NYC served in two directions between New York via Buffalo and Chicago. The NYC had a second line from Buffalo to Chicago via the north shore of Lake Erie and Detroit, Michigan. They had virtually no competition from any other rail line in the cities they served between New York and Buffalo.

The PRR had six very large cities along the route that they served in both directions, from New York via Philadelphia and Pittsburgh to Chicago. The PRR had a second line from Pittsburgh to Chicago through Columbus, Ohio. The PRR line southwest from New York to Philadelphia, Baltimore, and Washington, DC, was a virtual gold mine for them.

Even B&O, that took a roundabout route to Chicago via Philadelphia and Washington, DC, served eight large cities.

There were not many cities along the Erie main line whose metropolitan area reached 100,000 in population. The cities they served both east and west, were Paterson/Passaic, NJ; Binghamton, NY, and stretching a point, we will add Elmira, NY, and then Youngstown and Akron Ohio; a total of five larger markets.

Binghamton, and Elmira, New York, were also on the main line of the Delaware, Lackawanna and Western Railroad, which had shorter time schedules both to New York and Buffalo. The Erie shared the Youngstown and Akron, Ohio traffic with the B&O, which had faster trains to Chicago, and better trains to New York.

On the Erie main line you can throw out Patterson and Passaic, because a person going to Buffalo or Chicago could take an Erie train to Jersey City. There were other methods of transportation such as tube trains under the Hudson River, and the New York subway system to Pennsylvania, or Grand Central stations and a NYC train to Buffalo and Chicago, or a PRR train to Chicago. One could reach each destination much quicker than if they went by Erie direct to those two points.

None of the cities mentioned on the Erie were the size of Rochester, Buffalo, Cleveland or Detroit on the NYC; nor were they anywhere near the size of Philadelphia, Pittsburgh, Baltimore and Washington, DC on the PRR and B&O main lines. The Erie served Buffalo, and Cleveland, but only in one direction.

The distance on the Erie tracks from Jersey City to Chicago was 998 miles. The NYC from New York to Chicago did it in 960 miles, and the PRR an hour and a half less, at 902 miles. The B&O in its roundabout line through Washington, DC, to Chicago covered more than 1100 miles of rail. They outclassed the PRR for the passenger traffic from Washington DC to Chicago and points west on their line.

Index

Airborne Division 101st, 142.
Albany, NY, 5, 7, 8, 9, 32, 65, 115.
Atomic Bomb, 158.
Battle of the Bulge, 156.
Big Bands of the period, 142.
Binghamton, NY, 11, 15, 47, 51, 57, 66, 70, 78, 90, 91, 115, 116, 149, 161.
Castle Garden immigration station, 7, 8, 10.
Coyle, Anna, teacher, 86, 104, 107, 118.
Deaths or injury on the job:
   Angelo Tolomei, 61.
   Carmen Antonio Oropallo, 35, 36, 37, 38,39, 61, 61, 77, 78, 79.
   Salvatore Ficarro, 63.
   Salvatore Catalino, 63.
   Giovanni Oropallo, 62, 63.
Departments:
   Relief, 115.
   State, 139.
   War, 139.
DiVincenzo, Francis, T. 154.
Donnellan, P. M. Erie Supt.., 116.
Ellis Island, 7, 8, 11, 19, 37, 38, 46, 49, 80, 137, 138.
Erie Railway, 2, 9, 12, 13, 14, 15, 125.
Erie Railway's Day Express, 2, 12, 13, 14, 15.
Erie Railroad, 1, 2, 11, 12, 17, 19, 28, 29, 30, 32, 38, 39, 40, 41, 44, 46, 47, 49, 50, 58, 59, 61, 63, 64, 65, 66, 71, 74, 78, 79, 89, 90, 113, 115, 116, 117, 118, 121, 124, 125, 126, 132, 138, 143, 140, 145, 147, 148, 149, 151, 152, 153, 154, 156, 160, 161, 162.
Erie Limited, 63, 64, 121Photo, 125, 156, 158.
Erie Railroad train number 8 wreck, 90, 91.
Great Depression, 1, 2, 66-74, 89, 90, 95, 101, 126, 128, 151.
Grillo, Salvatore, 123Photo. 135, 136, 141, 142.
Grillo, Jimmy, 150.
Hancock, NY, 13.

Infantry Division 104th (The Timberwolves), 141, 142, 156.
Italian internment, 137, 138, 139.
Italian soldiers:
   Said miracle, 23.
   In North Africa, 140.
Iwo Jima, 141.
Japanese Internment, 137, 138, 139.
Jewish death camps, 139.
Kemp, Miss, teacher, 1, 127, 128.
Lanning, Miss, teacher, 86, 103, 104, 118.
Little Italy, 2, 19, 20, 38, 46, 48, 130
Lucecco, Tody, 142.
Madonna Della Libera, 19, 22, 23, 27, 52Photo. 58.
Mango:
   Uncle Bernardino, 22, 24, 25, 26, 27, 28, 29, 35, 38, 41, 60, 66, 159.
   First Cousin Chuck/Angelo, 48,, 72, 77, 81, 111, 114, 122Photo.141, 142, 156.
   First cousin Frank, 72, 77, 81, 112, 114, 122/124photos, 141, 156.
   Giovannina 1st named, 50, 55/56Photo, 58, 59, 60.
   Giovannina 2nd named, 60, 70, 71, 72, 73, 75, 76, 77, 78, 82, 83, 87, 89, 91,120Photo.
   First Cousin Jack, 72, 81, 82, 111, 114, 122Photo.
   First cousin Joseph, 141, 142
   Zi Pasquale, 22, 25, 26, 27, 28, 31, 32, 33, 34, 35, 39, 40, 42, 48, 57, 60, 67, 72, 73, 81, 82, 83, 93, 107, 111, 114, 122photo, 159.
Missoula, Montana, 138.
Muck Land, 135.
Mulberry Street, 2, 19, 20, 38, 46, 48, 130.
Murphy, Catherine, teacher, 86, 87, 88, 107.
Nemo, Mr., Union leader, 149.
Newspapers:
   Binghamton Leader, 15.
   Hornell Evening Tribune, 142.
   Susquehanna Transcript, 69, 107.

Index

Oropallo, Billy, 76, 77, 104.
Oropallo, Fiore, 5, 29, 30, 36, 62.
Oropallo, Giovanni, 62, 63, 76, 104.
Our Lady of Fatima, 22, 23.
Our Lady of Lourdes, 22, 23.
Our Lady of Freedom Moiano, 22, 23, 52Photo, 58.
Prospect Street, 612 home 120photo.
Railroads, 1922 national strike 48, 50, 161, 162.
Robert Packer Hospital, Sayre, PA, 71, 116, 117.
Rockwell, William O. 154.
Roosevelt, (FDR) 89, 111, 137, 138, 139, 158.
Schenectady, NY, 33, 39, 72, 111, 114, 115, 118, 133, 141, 145, 156.
Slavic immigrants, 11.
Sons of Italy, 41, 42, 50, 104.
Sons of Italy, 57band photo.
Steamships:
  Conte Bianca Mane, S. S., 135.
  Principe Di Piemonte, S. S., 35, 37,

54Photo.
  Dante Alighieri, S. S., 47, 54Photo.
Sexton, Shorty, 149, 150, 151.
Susquehanna Depot, PA, 11, 13, 14, 17.
Timberwolves (104 Infantry Division), 141, 142, 156.
Truman, President, 158.
Whalen, Buddy, 134, 135.
World War One, 6, 8, 21, 22, 41.
World War Two, 72, 85, 125, 127, 140, 127, 140, 158.